THIS BOOK BELONGS TO

Fiona Y. Scholes

In producing this book, I should like to thank Julian
Barker for his help and vigilance, Colorsport for contributing
to picture research, and Ian Smith and Robin Sheppard for
providing material that stirred great memories.

Published by:
The Bluecoat Press
Bluecoat Chambers
School Lane
Liverpool L1 3BX

Designed by:
March design
Origination:
Oriel Studios
Printed by:
Stanley Printing Company
Photographs by:
Colorsport

ISBN 1 872568 29 7

Leeds United
The Glory Years

The Triumph and Tumult of the Revie Era

Andrew Mourant

THE BLUECOAT PRESS

INTRODUCTION

One man's insatiable ambition and the willingness of another to back him to the hilt fashioned Leeds United's turbulent years of success in the 1960s and 1970s. Such was the chemistry between manager Don Revie and the club's millionaire chairman Harry Reynolds, men from humble backgrounds with a sharp eye for opportunity and the abundance of energy that makes things happen. Revie, at 33, was in his twilight years as a player at Leeds United and seeking his first break in management at Bournemouth when Reynolds realised, while writing a testimonial, that he was in danger of off-loading one of the club's few precious assets. With the decisive turn of mind that can make fortunes, Reynolds tore up the letter and offered Revie the vacant job at Leeds. Thus it was that on 15 March 1961, an extraordinary soccer revolution was born.

The character of Don Revie intrigued many. Few found it possible to be neutral about him. He was a cultured player yet he unleashed into English league football one of the most aggressive teams it had ever known. He was invariably civil, had a yearning to be liked, yet succeeded in offending football officials and some fellow managers throughout his career. His attention to detail was fanatical yet his moods and instincts swayed by superstition. He had grandiose ambitions for his football team yet often exhorted them to be cautious at all costs. Perhaps that was born of insecurity. Born in July, 1927, in Middlesbrough, Revie, the youngest of three children, came to know much about hardship and clinging on to what little you had. In the Depression, his father, a joiner, spent two years unemployed. The family took in washing to earn extra money. Revie's later boyhood became clouded with a profound sadness: his mother died of cancer in 1939 leaving her 12-year-old son desolate. Don Revie turned to football for consolation, practising ball control in almost all his spare time.

The game had been his passion since the age of six, when his father first took him to see Middlesbrough play. Afterwards, a bundle of rags at his feet, he would try to mimic goal-scoring feats of his first player-hero, George Camsell and, at the age of nine, young Don Revie was picked to play for Archibald School at outside-right. It was the start of a great career. After leaving school at 14 to become an apprentice bricklayer, Revie progressed through Newport Boys Club to the illustrious local team, Middlesbrough Swifts, where he began to attract professional scouts and, in July 1944, to Leicester City. There, and thereafter with Hull City, Manchester City, Sunderland and Leeds, he embarked on a playing career that lasted 17 seasons, saw him win six England caps and voted Footballer of the Year in 1955.

Revie was a polite, urbane, cerebral footballer, fascinated by tactics. There was little sign of the driven man who became the controversial figurehead of Leeds United. Raich Carter, his manager at Hull City, said: "I think he let me down. He didn't have the punch an inside-forward should." The complexion Revie took on as a manager also astonished Carter: "I didn't think he was aggressive enough." There was a sense among those who knew Don Revie – Carter included - that the desire to make as much money as possible contributed to his restlessness, his wandering among five clubs. There was also a sense that he was constantly exhorted by his wife Elsie (niece of Johnny Duncan, Revie's manager at Leicester City) to make the best of himself financially and socially. As a boy brought up in Middlesbrough during the 1920s and '30s, Revie had an uncomfortable remembrance of hard times. Yet the offer of riches never tempted him away from Elland Road. While the threat of going elsewhere generally secured him a better deal, Revie's relationship with Leeds United was never solely about money.

Along with Harry Reynolds, he had moulded Leeds in the image of a large family. It was to families, at home and at work, that Revie clung, in search of the warmth that his later childhood had lacked. He was utterly determined to do what he felt was best for his families. Often it was painful. Sometimes he was ruthless. This is the story of his travails for his football family and theirs for him, and their battles with the outside world during thirteen tempestuous years.

An unbeatable combination. Don Revie training with inspirational team captain Billy Bremner.

When Don Revie took over from Jack Taylor as manager at Leeds United, the club was broke and morale was low. There were few past glories from which to draw inspiration: Leeds had won no trophy of note apart from the second division championship. Although Harry Reynolds had been much impressed by Revie's thoughtful attitude towards the game, the new Leeds manager was appointed as much in hope as in expectation. Yet had Harry Reynolds not mulled over the situation and posted those glowing references off to Bournemouth instead . . . Even now, more than 30 years later, the prospect is enough to make Leeds United fans with long memories shudder. Amid the prevailing aimlessness at Elland Road, it is hard to imagine that any manager would have dedicated his life to reconstructing Leeds United with the commitment that Revie did. He had extravagant visions. Probably he needed them: the reality of Leeds' position was almost too wretched to contemplate otherwise. He changed Leeds' strip from a gloomy blue and old gold to all white, the colours of Real Madrid, the greatest club team in Europe during the late 1950s and early '60s. Visions tend to visit madmen, mystics or geniuses. Revie was to prove a genius at football management, yet one flawed by a susceptibility to bizarre superstitions. Once he summoned a gypsy from Scarborough to Elland Road so that she might drive out the curse he believed was blighting his team's fortunes.

To begin with, Leeds United's ascent was neither inevitable nor inexorable. In 1961/62, Revie's first full season in charge, Leeds United endured, judged by results alone, the worst season in their 43-year history: 19th in division two, avoiding relegation to the third division for the first time by a whisker. It had been a desperate campaign but, with the arrival of Harry Reynolds as chairman in 1961, money was available to buy. It was, according to coach Syd Owen, a race against time. "We had to get some mature, professional players to stabilise the position until the young ones came through." To be sure of survival, Leeds needed a point from their last game of the season at Newcastle. What if they had lost? Could Revie have dragged them back from the third division? Would he have still been in the job? As it turned out, the team mastered a bone-dry pitch and blustery conditions to produce their most assured performance of a desperate season. That 3-0 victory was a turning point in their history: it confirmed a growing belief that the worst was over and there was a platform for revival.

Of all the mature players Revie invested in, one key figure lay behind the stiffened resolve that saw Leeds United lose only one of their last eleven league games. Bobby Collins, suddenly out of favour at Everton, had been signed by Revie in March 1962. The diminutive Scottish inside-forward arrived at Elland Road with a sense of wounded pride and a ferocious desire to prove to the world that, at 31, he still had much to offer. "I came back from training and Don Revie, Harry Reynolds and Manny Cussins (another member of the Leeds board) were waiting on the doorstep. I was impressed by just how much they wanted me." Collins' appetite for the game was boundless; his experience gained from twelve years at the top, including 28 games for Scotland, invaluable. Never was the £25,000 he cost Leeds United better spent. Aside from his technical accomplishments – a great ability to read the game, to strike penetrating long balls, shoot with fiendish power and tackle with a fierceness that left much larger men gasping – Collins had a passion for the game that rubbed off on lesser team-mates.

Amid all the anxieties and traumas, there were glimpses of young talent. Revie's much disparaged predecessors, Bill Lambton and Jack Taylor, had begun working on a youth policy that later would be developed and exploited to brilliant effect. Almost from the moment that he made his debut at Chelsea on 23 January 1960, it was clear that Billy Bremner, then aged

Above. An outcast full of fight: Bobby Collins, snubbed by Everton, joined Revie's Leeds at the age of 31 with the club at its lowest ebb. His leadership was a driving force in the revival at Elland Road.
Opposite. Uncontainable at centre-forward, stopper supreme at centre-half. For many, John Charles was Leeds United before the rise of Don Revie's team.

Above. In control: under Don Revie, Jack Charlton metamorphosed from erratic centre-half to World Cup winner. A giant in Leeds United's glory years, he played a record 773 matches for the club.

Below. Maurice Lindley, the affable assistant manager. He's in jacket and tie between Partridge and Owen.

seventeen and playing at outside-right, had marked ability. Yet he was not a Revie discovery. It was Revie's management of the young Scot's volatile temperament through encouragement, and later making him captain, that saw Bremner evolve from raw talent into a world-class midfield player. And it was Revie's intense persuasiveness that persuaded him to stay. For Bremner was homesick, pining for his girlfriend Vicky. "The gaffer went up to Stirling to speak to her parents. I couldn't believe it, he was saying maybe it would be better if Vicky came down to England which is really something he should never have done," Bremner recalled. When there was talk of selling Bremner to Everton, Revie threatened a walk-out, for it was around the bellicose Scot that the Leeds manager intended building his team.

The pre-Revie youth policy had also discovered the gangling, skinny, 15-year-old Norman Hunter who, though equipped with fine footballing instincts, lacked the strength to place passes where he wanted them – unimaginable to the strikers he dispossessed so forcefully after he blossomed into one of Britain's most unyielding defenders. Yet, amid the uncertainty and lack of purpose at Elland Road, Hunter nearly drifted away. Signing him was one of Revie's first acts as manager.

One figure among the old guard had to be sorted out: Jack Charlton, who made his debut in 1953 and had played regularly at the heart of the Leeds defence since 1955. Charlton was proving an awkward character, often at odds with himself and the world, and a firm believer that he always knew best. Over the years, his performances had been notoriously inconsistent. Charlton was fast, a superb header of the ball and a crisp, clean tackler; good enough to have played for the Football League against the League of Ireland in 1957 but as Leeds United declined, so Charlton's performances became wayward. Often, he appeared to make up his own game plan as matches progressed. While Revie never quite eliminated all Charlton's eccentricities, he did drum into him the need to mark opposing centre-forwards much more tightly though, as Norman Hunter recalled: "Big Jack never liked being told what to do." Above all, Revie made it plain who was in charge at Elland Road and Charlton's performances for the next ten years suggested that, as much as anything, the dearth of strong leadership at Elland Road had arrested his development. Few footballing careers have flowered so spectacularly in their latter stages as did that of Jack Charlton.

Just as he inherited the talents of Bremner, Charlton and Hunter, the backroom staff that served Revie consistently for twelve seasons was also in place: assistant manager and chief scout Maurice Lindley, a former Everton centre-half, coach Syd Owen, the former Luton Town

and England centre-half and trainer Les Cocker, who had played as a forward with Stockport; all had come to Elland Road in July 1960, when Jack Taylor was manager. Bob English, the physiotherapist, had joined the club in 1957 when Raich Carter was manager. Owen's meticulous attention to detail and Cocker's sometimes pitiless training sessions, which helped make Leeds United players among the fittest in the country, were key factors in the reconstruction.

In the 1962/63 season, there were clear signs that a revival of Leeds United's fortunes was underway. It was to be a campaign disrupted by the bitter winter: so intense was the big freeze that the first football of the new year could not be played until March. While for Leeds United the gala event of the season was the return from Italy of John Charles – perhaps the most complete footballer ever to have played for the club – the more significant and successful developments were low-key. Indeed, the return of Charles to Elland Road from Juventus was a flop. He had served Leeds United magnificently in the 1950s at centre-half and centre-forward but now lacked any appetite for toiling in the second division. After eleven games, Charles returned to Italy, to Roma, for £65,000 – a deal that netted the club a quick £12,000 profit. The season and the long-term future were to be shaped by young players who cost nothing.

The team that took the field against Swansea on 8 September 1962 contained names which, while unfamiliar at the time, were to become inseparable from Leeds United's greatest achievements. A feeble performance in the 2-1 home defeat by Bury three days previously prompted Revie to introduce three débutants: Norman Hunter, then 18, Paul Reaney, 17, and Rod Johnson, also 17. Though Johnson scored, it was his misfortune to be carried off with an injury and his career never flourished at Elland Road. But Hunter and Reaney, having made their breakthrough, were there to stay. The backbone of the side that day, which won 2-0, was: Sprake, Reaney, Mason, Bremner, Charlton, Hunter. It was almost unchanged nine seasons later; the team that ran out against Liverpool at Elland Road on 18 September 1971, and was by then unquestionably the finest in Britain, had as its nucleus: Sprake, Reaney, Cooper, Bremner, Charlton, Hunter. Liverpool, meanwhile, who with Leeds were the most consistent side of that era, had new personnel in each of those six positions.

Revie had worried about blooding his young men at Swansea because he feared they were unready for the rigours of the second division. Their durability and the speed at which they learned the game must have exceeded his wildest expectations. Chivvied by Bobby Collins, Leeds United began to acquire a reputation for being hard to beat and awkward to play

Above. Poise, balance and determination: a classic study of Billy Bremner in action. Below. They shall not pass: but Norman Hunter, a debutant in 1962 with Paul Reaney, often turned creator as well as destroyer. The formidable Hunter also played more than 700 matches and won 28 England caps.

against. They finished fifth and so upbeat was their form through March and April 1963 that they were spoken of as promotion possibles. But inside and outside the club it was felt that consistency was lacking, that the team lacked cunning.

In signing Johnny Giles at the beginning of 1963/64, Revie acquired a footballer who came to epitomise craft, guile and trickery. Giles arrived at Elland Road having finished the previous season an FA Cup winner with Manchester United. But he claimed to be disaffected by internal squabbles at Old Trafford, unsure of his ability to command a first-team place and, above all, impressed by Revie's ambition. "Leeds had had a good run the previous season but Don Revie was a big factor and had learned from his playing days all the faults of managers", said Giles. But for all his abundant skill and speed, Giles was not quite the finished article. He had not perfected the art of making the long, penetrative passes for which he became renowned: this came two seasons later when circumstances forced Revie to switch him to midfield. He was not yet the sometimes ruthless operator feared by so many opponents but a single campaign exposed to Revie's fierce will to win helped change that. In Collins, Bremner and Giles, none of whom measured more than five feet five, Revie had assembled a formidable triumvirate of players with an abundance of skill and aggression.

With a strong showing in the previous year from which to draw confidence, Leeds United set about the 1963/64 season with a stern sense of purpose. They were desperate for promotion and other teams bore the bruises to prove it. Clashes with promotion rivals Sunderland and Preston were especially abrasive, marred by violent play and running feuds among the players. Yet, says Johnny Giles, Leeds were tactically naive, at least to start with. Early in the season, they had tried to outplay Derby County by playing sweet football, only to find themselves 2-0 down at half-time. During the interval, Revie lambasted his troops and ordered them to revert to their hustling style, never allowing the opposition to settle. They did so and pulled back to draw 2-2.

Few could live with Leeds' tireless pursuit of success. In becoming second division champions, they lost only three of 42 league matches. A consistent, settled side, in which each man battled for the other, was the key: nine of Revie's team played in 35 games or more and, although a number of their games were dour encounters, the presence of South African-born Albert Johanneson on the left wing provided some scintillating moments. On form, Johanneson could reduce any defence to a shambles with his darting runs and trickery. He arrived at Elland Road in April 1961, a few weeks after Revie took over as manager, and became a regular in 1962/63 but his nine seasons at Elland Road were clouded by self-doubt. Wingers cannot be expected to perform miracles in every match yet far too often Johanneson, who was always diffident and sometimes the butt of racial abuse, failed to do his talents justice. The 1963/64 season was possibly his finest. Johanneson, much mourned following his untimely death in September 1995 at the age of 55, was one of those players of whom fans who saw him say: "Do you remember when Albert did . . . ?" And he was capable of brilliance on the big stage. For Leeds United, few games were more important than the encounter with Newcastle United on Easter Monday 1964 when Johanneson killed a long through ball and left three opponents in his wake before slipping the ball past the advancing goalkeeper. That goal gave Leeds a priceless 2-1 victory. Johanneson hit 13 league goals in 1963/64 when goals for Leeds were scarce: they failed to score more than twice in any league match from 2 November to 7 March. The shy South African was joint top scorer with Don Weston, a fit, fast and mobile striker who often caught defences on the hop by launching attacks from midfield.

It was clear as the season reached its climax that Leeds United's promotion challenge could founder through an inability to score. With his other principal striker, Ian Lawson, losing form and confidence, Revie paid out £55,000 – then a club record – to bring England international Alan Peacock from Middlesbrough to Elland Road. It was another of the Leeds manager's sound investments: Peacock was big, brave and a marvellous header of the ball, valued as much for the chances he created as for his goals.

Peacock's arrival seemed to free up Leeds United's stuttering attack. The team won eight and drew two of its last ten matches, shaking off all other pretenders to the second division crown. Promotion was secured with a 3-0 win at Swansea on 11 April; the title with a 2-0 win at Charlton in the final game of the season. Never would a leaner, meaner young team be unleashed on the first division. For Revie's men had arrived not to serve but to conquer and were to leave an indelible impression on their new environment.

Opposite above. Passes from Johnny Giles had the accuracy of guided missiles. The Irish midfielder had an unmatched genius for outwitting the opposition and unlocking defences.
Opposite below. Almost too brave for his own good – Alan Peacock was a fearless centre-forward who added weight and power to the Leeds attack. A fine header of the ball, successive knee injuries brought Peacock's career to a premature end.
Left. None fitter or hungrier: the Leeds United squad 1963/64, destined to be second division champions.
Above. Speed, bewildering ball control but sometimes lacking self-belief. When in the mood, South African Albert Johanneson could reduce any defence to a shambles.

"We were no worse than other clubs. Chelsea had a very hard side; Everton, Liverpool. That's the way the game was played then. Don never told us to rough it up. He knew he had people, Paul Reaney and Norman Hunter, who liked to play it that way."

Peter Lorimer

Leeds United marked their return to the first division with three consecutive victories. If those games had been lost, the history not only of the 1964/65 season but also the next ten years might have been very different. Johnny Giles was convinced that this early success buoyed up the team for the rest of the season. Revie's men could outrun and outfight almost any opponents but were still green and an early sequence of poor results might have dented their confidence irreparably.

Revie's extravagant talk of winning the league title seemed less outlandish when, in early September, Leeds sat on top of the first division. They wouldn't have been the first newcomers to arrive with a blaze of form, only to fade once a lack of strength in depth was exposed or good teams got their measure. When, in the next eight league matches, Leeds lost four, drew two and managed only two victories, it looked as if they were being cut down to size.

It was clear that if the route to success was about battles of will and trials of strength, Revie's men would not buckle easily. An FA report revealed that the previous season Leeds United had earned more cautions – 18 – than any other team in the Football League, albeit that many were incurred by junior players. The reputation of Revie's men went before them but Leeds players of the era have always claimed that opponents provoked them deliberately and that Billy Bremner, especially, was singled out.

Was Leeds United's bad name justified? Peter Lorimer, whose career spanned over 20 years at Leeds, thinks not. "We were no worse than other clubs. Chelsea had a very hard side; Everton, Liverpool. That's the way the game was played then. Don never told us to rough it up. He knew he had people, Paul Reaney and Norman Hunter, who liked to play it that way." Billy Bremner says: "I've never known the gaffer say go out and kick them, or waste time. But we were young, we were cocky, and when we were away from home and scored, I can remember thinking that the people watching may as well go home there and then. We weren't contributing much to the entertainment."

Never was there a more rancorous game in the first division than Leeds' 1-0 win at Everton on 7 November. After their earlier dip in form, Leeds had steadied themselves and had come to Goodison with four straight wins behind them. A bad, late tackle on Jack Charlton immediately after kick-off set the pattern of a match so vicious, so full of running battles, and so inflammatory that, ten minutes before half-time, referee Roger Stokes took the players off the field to try to cool things down. Players continued feuding until the final whistle. "It was diabolical; they blamed us, yet some Everton players were going over the ball time and time again," says Bobby Collins. "You can't turn the other cheek or they'll kill you." However much Everton were to blame, the match helped give Leeds a notoriety for foul play that they never quite managed to relinquish throughout the Revie era.

Yet that era had looked likely to end the previous month when first the Leeds manager accepted and then changed his mind over a lucrative offer to take over at Sunderland. With the air clear and the prospect of continued stability, Leeds hit peak form, winning seven successive league matches. The run ended with a 3-1 defeat at West Ham on 21 November but that seemed of little consequence as Revie's men went unbeaten for a further eighteen matches and were yoked together with Manchester United and Chelsea in the race for the championship.

Discipline, method, application, aggression, caution: such were the qualities by which Leeds United had clawed their way from the second division twilight zone to the threshold of the League Championship, a prize they had not been remotely near in their history. The same will to win gave them the momentum to make unprecedented progress in the FA Cup and, at

Head and shoulders above everyone: Jack Charlton's aerial domination puts Liverpool goalkeeper Tommy Lawrence under pressure in the 1965 FA Cup Final . . .

the beginning of April 1965, Leeds, who had previously never been beyond the quarter-finals, were not only on top of the first division but also Wembley-bound.

As with their voyage through the first division, Leeds' passage in the Cup precipitated some stormy encounters. In the sixth-round tie at Crystal Palace, the home side were under orders to be as unflinching as their opponents. It made for a ferocious first half but Leeds had expertise as well as muscle, and scored three goals without reply after the interval. The first of two semi-final matches against Manchester United, played at Hillsborough on a heavy pitch, was another in which desperadoes came out on top and football a distant second; a match of many bruises, three bookings and no goals.

The replay at the City Ground, Nottingham, was equally hard-fought but more fluid and less brutal. It was also a night on which Revie's young team showed a remarkable capacity for soaking up pressure. This clash between the top two teams in the league defined a vivid contrast in styles: Manchester United's appetite for pressing forward with flair wherever possible and Leeds' policy of building on solid defence and counter-attacking to relieve pressure.

Almost when they looked ready to crack, Leeds made a tactical switch, unleashing Bremner – who had begun his career as a forward – into the attack for the last twenty minutes. Slowly Leeds began to exert a grip and, three minutes from time, Bremner's flashing header settled the game. This was the pinnacle of Leeds' season and achieved without adding to the nucleus of players who, last season, had been contesting the second division.

To a man, they had made astonishing progress. Willie Bell, automatic choice at left-back for the past two campaigns, had arrived at Leeds from Queen's Park in 1960. A mediocre-looking midfielder who couldn't get a regular game even when Leeds were struggling, he switched to defence with the departures of Grenville Hair, one of Leeds United's great servants, and Cliff Mason; and more than made up for a shortage of pace with bravery, anticipation and heading ability. The extent of Bell's transformation into a top-class defender was underlined when he was capped by Scotland in 1966.

Centre-forward Jim Storrie was another unflashy, reliable Scotsman from whom Revie extracted the maximum. Signed for £15,000 from Airdrie in 1962, his arrival was overshadowed by the fleeting return of John Charles but what Storrie lacked in glamour and in height – he was under five feet nine – he compensated for with selfless hard-running, a sharp eye for goal and the knack of disturbing defences to create chances for team-mates. In 156 games for Leeds, Storrie scored 67 goals – an excellent strike rate.

When Alan Peacock was fit, he was a formidable presence in the Leeds attack but such was his commitment to the cause, he all too frequently launched himself into dangerous places where bodies were thrashing and boots flying. Injury-prone at Middlesbrough, Peacock's troublesome knee continued to plague him at Elland Road. Leeds United's success in 1964/65 was all the more remarkable for having lacked Peacock's services until the campaign was three-quarters over. As in 1963/64, his late intervention coincided with the team scoring more profusely than at any other time in the campaign.

Gary Sprake, another Revie protégé, had made his début in the Leeds goal during the traumatic 1961/62 season when, just 16, he was airlifted to Southampton as an emergency replacement after Tommy Younger had been taken ill. Of much greater significance was his second appearance a few months later alongside debutants Reaney, Hunter and Johnson at Swansea. As with Reaney and Hunter, that game marked for Sprake the beginning of an epic run in the Leeds first team: he would remain Revie's preferred goalkeeper for the next ten seasons.

The errors and lapses of concentration that Sprake's critics claim robbed Leeds of numerous trophies came later in his career. Selective memories and partial observers also forget that save for Sprake's contributions, Leeds might never have come as close to glory as often they did: Sprake alone had held Manchester United at bay in the 1964/65 FA Cup semi-final replay before his team-mates steadied, wrested control of the match, and then stole it at

Above. Left-back Grenville Hair was a composed and, when needed, ruthless full-back. A veteran of 474 matches he saw good and bad times but his career at Leeds ended in the second division championship season of 1963/64.

Opposite above. Once a mediocre wing-half, a move to left-back worked wonders for Willie Bell. A courageous, astute defender, he was capped twice by Scotland in 1966.

Opposite below. The FA Cup dream disintegrates. Gary Sprake is beaten as Liverpool take an extra-time lead at Wembley in the 1965 Cup Final.

the death. On the morning of 17 April 1965, Leeds United were poised to become only the second team to achieve the League and FA Cup double this century. Within three days, two shattering defeats, the first 1-0 at Elland Road against their principal adversaries Manchester United, dealt a blow from which Revie's team never recovered. Two days later they lost 3-0 at Sheffield Wednesday, playing as if all the fight had suddenly drained out of them.

The arithmetic shows that Manchester United won the league title only on goal average but that wicked little dip in form did irreversible damage before the final rites of Leeds' league season were acted out in a 3-3 draw at Birmingham on 26 April 1965. Statistics alone might suggest that Leeds' first appearance in an FA Cup Final against Liverpool was also close run. The scoreline records a 2-1 defeat with all the goals in extra time, the game finally settled by Ian St John in the 111th minute after Billy Bremner, against the run of play, equalised Roger Hunt's strike in the 93rd but rarely has a team appeared more leaden, less attuned to the big occasion than were Revie's men on a gloomy, overcast 1 May; and the narrow margin disguised the extent of their inferiority.

It was the day inexperience caught up with the young pretenders, almost as if Leeds United, players and fans alike, had been infected on the journey south to Wembley by lack of self-belief. Jack Charlton recalled arriving at the ground to see only a sea of Liverpool red and that the few Leeds fans he recognised had rosettes concealed inside their jackets. Jim Storrie recalled the team's agonising wait before kick-off. "In the tunnel we were biting our nails and just looking at Liverpool. It was terrible." The hero of a miserable final was Liverpool left-back Gerry Byrne, who played almost the entire match with a broken collar-bone. Revie's team relied too much on long high balls hit forward to Alan Peacock who was shut out of the game by the colossal Liverpool centre-half Ron Yeats. The skills of Albert Johanneson lay almost dormant: perhaps more than any Leeds player he was numbed by the occasion. The combative midfield duo of Collins and Bremner was constantly pushed back to help out a harassed defence. Defenders in general, and Sprake in particular, emerged with most credit for Leeds United on that sombre day.

After scaling hitherto unknown heights, Revie's fierce young team had wound up with nothing save the invaluable experience of sustained football combat at the top level. But they had the energy and spirit to bounce back from defeat. With a short summer of rest and driven on by the constant exhortations of Revie, Cocker and Owen, the players, a year stronger and wiser, threatened to be more formidable than ever.

> *"I think the dossiers made us pay the opposition too much respect.*
> *We analysed teams far too much."*
>
> *Norman Hunter*

No team ever knew more about its opponents than did Don Revie's Leeds United. Soccer tactics had fascinated Revie since his teenage days as a player with Middlesbrough Swifts who had paid Newport Boys Club five shillings (25 pence) for his services. Each Sunday, the Swifts reported to manager Bill Sanderson's house for a post-mortem on the previous day's match. Corks were used to represent players on a model pitch as Sanderson analysed mistakes and how things might be improved.

While only in his late 20s and at the peak of his playing career, Revie wrote his autobiography, *Soccer's Happy Wanderer*, devoting 20 pages to a discussion of tactics, especially the so-called Deep Revie Plan employed by Manchester City, of which he was the focal point. Inspired by the magnificent Hungarian team of the early 1950s, City manager Les McDowall fashioned a team that played around a deep-lying centre-forward, Revie, whose brief was to roam about the field as a provider and receiver of balls played to feet.

There was another mentor, Sep Smith, the Leicester City stalwart who took the 16-year-old Revie under his wing when he graduated from Middlesbrough Swifts in August 1944. Smith not only drove Revie to the limits of physical endurance – something that Revie's own young charges came to experience – he also taught the value of passing and running into position, the basis, according to Revie, of Manchester City's reorganisation in 1954/55.

Revie had seen order, method and planning in action and the success they could bring. Once appointed manager, his in-depth studies of opposing teams became legendary. The famous dossiers evolved by chance. One Saturday during the 1963/64 season, Revie had dispatched Syd Owen to look at a young player in whom he was interested. The thoroughness of Owen's written report was Revie's inspiration: henceforth, all Leeds United's opponents were to be put under surveillance, the findings dissected and training sessions arranged to devise the most effective tactics. A surfeit of knowledge could also bring about confusion, even fear of modest teams that Leeds should have knocked over simply through strength and ability. "I think the dossiers made us pay the opposition too much respect. We analysed teams far too much," reflected Norman Hunter. During the briefings that could last almost an hour, Billy Bremner's mind used to wander: "The only time I would listen was when he was talking about continental players I didn't know." Sometimes players were fearful of recriminations if, having forgotten or ignored Revie's briefings, they were outdone on the field. Few things made the Leeds manager more angry than seeing his hard work wasted.

The one new recruit to the Leeds set-up in 1965/66 was winger Mike O'Grady, returning to his home city after six years with Huddersfield Town where he had made rapid progress, winning an England cap against Northern Ireland shortly after his 20th birthday. Revie paid £45,000 for O'Grady, a buoyant, confident character who relished taking on defenders and was unabashed when he lost the ball. When on top form, O'Grady played with the air of a man who believed he was invincible. At his best, he very nearly was. He found training at Elland Road under Les Cocker a revelation. "At Huddersfield, if someone blew the whistle, it might take the players 10 minutes to get into line. At Leeds, it took 20 seconds, the training was so varied, sharp and well-organised."

From reserve-team football emerged more of Revie's extraordinary crop of youngsters who would change the face of the team. One was Peter Lorimer, Leeds United's youngest ever debutant when he first appeared in the 1-1 home draw against Southampton on 29 September 1962, aged 15 years and 289 days. However, he played only once in each of the following seasons before breaking through as a regular at inside-right in August 1965.

Like O'Grady, Lorimer had self-belief and also a phlegmatic, manageable temperament. He possessed probably the most powerful shot of any footballer of his generation, scoring goals

Opposite. Neat control, punishing crosses but above all a shot of legendary power: from 1962 to 1985, Peter Lorimer scored 237 goals for Leeds United in all competitions, a club record.
Above. *Skill and swagger: Mike O'Grady's vibrant form was a highlight of Leeds United's march to the League Championship in 1968/69.*

at an incredible rate when a junior player in Dundee. Revie won the scramble to sign him, racing overnight to Scotland and being stopped for speeding as he beat his rivals. With maturity, Lorimer became one of Leeds United's great acquisitions. His career covered two spells at the club and when it ended in 1985, more than 23 years after his debut, Lorimer had ousted John Charles as Leeds' all-time top scorer with a tally of 237 goals in 701 appearances. In his final years, Lorimer operated in midfield, passing on his expertise to a new generation of talented youngsters. During his heyday, he played on the right wing and, aside from his thunderous shooting, showed good pace, control and an ability to wrong-foot defences with punishingly accurate crosses.

Jimmy Greenhoff, another fine, fluent young player who found his best position when converted from midfield to forward, had to wait a further season for regular first-team football. An excellent striker of the ball with an assured first touch, many Leeds fans mourned the passing of Greenhoff's talents when he was sold to Birmingham City in 1968, disappointed at his inability to command an automatic place in the Leeds line-up.

For the first half of the 1965/66 season, Revie's men were again serious championship contenders, confirming that their precocious showing in the previous campaign was no fluke. But in October, a change of profound significance was forced upon them following their first venture abroad in European competition. Leading 2-1 from the home match of their Inter Cities Fairs Cup tie against the Italian side Torino, in the return leg, Bobby Collins was flattened by a tackle so brutal that it broke his right thigh. Although showing great guts to fight back and make a fleeting return to the first team seven months later, Collins never regained an automatic place and the injury led ultimately to his departure from Elland Road.

As player and motivator, his value to the team had been incalculable. Collins could not easily be replaced and the one player Revie was desperate to sign, Blackpool's indefatigable young midfielder Alan Ball, would always elude him. Instead, Revie switched Johnny Giles from the right flank to Collins' role. From there, Giles evolved into a world-class schemer, lacking nothing, least of all the devil, shown by his predecessor. Jack Charlton, meanwhile, whose form was now so consistent that it had earned him his first England cap the previous season, assumed the captaincy.

European competition introduced Leeds United to new levels of ferocity on the football field. If any team was unlikely to wilt in the face of brutality and gamesmanship, it was Revie's Leeds. Despite the loss of Collins, they had conquered Torino 2-1 on aggregate and, after beating the East German side SC Leipzig by the same margin, faced the Spanish team Valencia in the third round.

Even by Leeds' standards the first leg, a 1-1 draw at Elland Road, was a tempestuous affair, with Jack Charlton at the eye of the storm. For once Charlton lost all self-control after being kicked, then punched, as he challenged for a high ball in the Valencia penalty area. When a mêlée of players squared up to each other, the Dutch referee Leo Horn was able to regain control only after taking both sets of players off the field for 11 minutes. The chief protagonists, Charlton and Valencia full-back Garcia Ridagany, were sent off and, before 90 minutes were up, Valencia inside-forward Sanchez-Lage was also dismissed for kicking Jim Storrie.

Mayhem had a habit of following Revie's men around. In successive seasons, referees had resorted to taking Leeds players off the pitch as a last resort before they, or their opponents, brought the house down. But for each match disfigured by brawling, there were performances of great self-discipline, particularly away from home. The return leg against Valencia, for which lurid predictions had been made, was a case in point: a trouble-free football match in which Leeds' concentration never wavered and victory came from a smartly taken goal by Mike O'Grady following a swift counter-attack. Although in the fourth round Leeds took a 4-1 lead to their Hungarian opponents Ujpest Dosza, Revie's men found themselves by-passed for much of the away game by slick, short, inter-passing movements. Another message was reinforced: stick to the man, don't chase the ball around. A 1-1 draw flattered Leeds' bemused performance.

Real Zaragoza, their Spanish opponents in the semi-final, had all Valencia's meanness but also uncontainable talent. Just as Charlton had been battered by Valencia, Giles was singled out for rough treatment in the first leg at Zaragoza and finally sent off for retaliation four minutes from time, along with his persecutor Violeta. Until then Leeds had shown self-control and defensive skill, conceding only a penalty goal against one of Europe's finest club sides. After a 2-1 victory at Elland Road, secured by goals from Johanneson and Charlton, it took a play-off, also held at Leeds, to settle the tie. But within thirteen minutes Zaragoza had carved the Leeds defence to pieces and were 3-0 up. Jimmy Greenhoff limped through most of the rest of the match with an ankle injury and Charlton's goal in the second half came too late to rescue the match.

At home, the season provided less drama, with anti-climactic early exits from both knock-out competitions: a 1-0 defeat at Chelsea in the fourth round of the FA Cup and a 4-2 defeat at Elland Road by West Bromwich Albion in round three of the League Cup. Although Leeds were the main contenders in the league, Revie's championship ambitions were severely deflated when on 28 December they lost 1-0 at home to Liverpool, their principal rivals in the title race. Liverpool roared into their best form of the season, winning six and drawing one of the next seven matches. By late February, Bill Shankly's team appeared uncatchable and won the league with 61 points – the same number achieved by Leeds and Manchester United the previous season – but six ahead of Leeds in 1965/66.

At the start of 1966/67, and for the first time since the Revie revolution, there was a sense that for all their strenuous efforts, Leeds United did not quite know the way forward. Their form over the first three months of the season was more faltering than at any time since Revie had taken over; only 23 goals were scored in the first 19 league matches. A 7-0 humiliation away at West Ham United in the League Cup on 7 November was followed, despite Revie's angry demands that nothing like it must ever recur, by a 5-0 drubbing at Liverpool twelve days later.

Alan Peacock's persistent injuries were part of the problem for there was no-one else to shoulder the striker's burden. Having played just over half the previous season's league matches until forced to leave the field during Leeds' 2-0 away defeat at Sunderland on 29 January, Peacock made only a smattering of appearances in 1966/67 before transferring to Plymouth Argyle. Supporters grew restive, for they saw no evidence of Revie striving to find a replacement. Auxiliaries were tried: Jimmy Greenhoff and, on occasions, Rod Belfitt; but while Greenhoff had finesse and Belfitt a neat touch with a sharp eye for goal, neither had the clout of a fully-fit Peacock.

It would have been unfair to blame stand-in goalkeeper David Harvey for the 7-0 hammering at West Ham. At Liverpool, where Leeds were scarcely any better, the seasoned rearguard of Sprake, Reaney, Bell, Bremner, Charlton and Hunter were on parade. Yet such massive defeats, unprecedented in the Revie era, proved aberrations rather than symptoms of a crisis. After the debacle at Anfield, Leeds lost only four of their remaining 26 first division matches and worked up a head of steam in both the FA Cup and Inter Cities Fairs Cup.

Despite the want of a commanding figure to lead the attack, more of Revie's protégés were blossoming. Paul Madeley, who had made his début at centre-half in 1963/64, had a rare versatility. As his team-mates became injured, Madeley emerged from the reserves to fill one position after another: by the end of 1966/67, he had made 27 league appearances and appeared everywhere other than in goal and at inside-left.

Madeley holds a unique place in football history. While never holding down a position he could call his own, his talents were so indispensable that when his career at Leeds ended in 1980, he had made 724 appearances in all competitions and been capped by England 24 times. Strength, elegance and coolness were his trademarks. Although Madeley originally came into the side as a centre-half and looked at one stage a likely replacement for Jack Charlton, the debate persisted over his best position. Possibly he excelled most when forti-fying midfield, winning the ball with an assured tackle and sweeping forward like a limousine in overdrive.

Opposite above. The knack of filling-in: striker Rod Belfitt, though never a regular first choice centre-forward, gave Leeds sterling service over eight years, scoring 33 goals in 104 matches.
Above. Few better, none more versatile: Paul Madeley filled every position except goal for Leeds United. The ultimate utility player, he made more than 700 appearances and earned 24 caps in 17 seasons at Elland Road.

Above. The greatest of them all? Injuries blighted Eddie Gray's long career at Elland Road but when fit, he showed world-class skills on the left wing.

Opposite. Much more than a defender: despite his conversion from winger to left-back, Terry Cooper's overlapping runs were a potent attacking weapon.

Don Revie was even less sure about how best to accommodate another of his young stars, Terry Cooper. For all his adroit control and passing ability, the left-sided Cooper was not a straightforward footballer. He looked too slow and lacking in sharpness to function as a winger and, with his appearances coming in fits and starts, grew increasingly restless at Elland Road. Knowing that he wanted to keep Cooper, yet not knowing how best to exploit his ability, was a headache for Revie. In the background hovered Blackburn Rovers, watching Cooper's unease with great interest, but they would not meet Leeds' £25,000 asking price. Cooper's career took a decisive turn the following season when Revie tried him at left-back in place of Willie Bell. What Cooper lacked in speed and the knack of stopping burly attackers in their tracks, Norman Hunter, acting as his shield, could supply. From a much deeper position, and facing play, Cooper had licence to help construct attacking moves and embark on adventures upfield by overlapping on the wing. In this tailor-made role, Cooper helped give Leeds' play a more fluent and attractive dimension.

However ugly some of Leeds United's performances were in the interests of avoiding defeat, Don Revie remained passionate about attracting youthful talent. It was miraculous that his management and scouting system had lured the cream of British talent to such an unfashionable club. Chief among Revie's prizes was Eddie Gray, whose technique and ball control were without equal at Leeds and probably matched only by George Best of Manchester United. Revie and Syd Owen had first sight of Gray in 1963 when the young Glaswegian was 15, playing for Scotland schoolboys. They were stunned by his extravagant gifts. Owen, not noted for exaggeration, recalled: "We could hardly believe what we were seeing." They were not alone: around 30 clubs were striving to sign Gray but none, when it came to a contest involving charm and determination, proved a match for Don Revie, who believed that Scotland contained the finest raw football talent in Britain. In England, he felt, the boys who grew up hungry for football were no longer around; it was his belief that higher standards of living had blunted their appetite.

Eddie Gray was an unmistakable figure when on the ball. With shoulders hunched and a graceful, loping run, his dribbling skills enabled him to thread intricate patterns through and around bemused defenders. Of the two scourges notorious for undermining football genius, namely a wayward temperament or injury, the latter was to blight Gray's progress. Although he served Leeds with grace and distinction for 20 years, a chronic thigh problem forced Gray to remain a bystander during many of the club's finest moments. He made a scoring debut in Leeds' 3-0 home victory against Sheffield Wednesday on New Year's Day 1966, and in 1966/67 forced his way into the first team, making 29 league appearances.

Gray's sparkling play was a feature of Leeds' consistently improved form when, after a fits and starts first three months, the team began its habitual pursuit of honours. Like some magical elixir, the FA Cup sent energy and optimism surging through Elland Road. Following decisive home wins in round three against Crystal Palace (3-0) and round four against West Bromwich Albion (5-0), three feverish encounters with Sunderland in round five drew more than 154,000 spectators. After a 1-1 draw at Roker Park on 11 March, four days later fans stampeded to Elland Road for a replay that had not been made all-ticket. The match, another 1-1 draw, attracted the biggest home crowd – 57,892 – in Leeds United's history, 18 of whom were injured on the Lowfields Road terraces when a crush barrier gave away. Development of the ground had lagged behind the club's rapid ascent; overcrowding on this scale was the stuff of potential calamity. Revie's team won the second rancorous replay at Hull 2-1, in which two Sunderland men were sent off. Ticket arrangements were more orderly for the sixth-round home tie against Manchester City and one goal, scored by Jack Charlton, delivered victory and a second semi-final in three years.

The nature of their semi-final defeat against Chelsea at Villa Park on 29 April 1967 was a foretaste of things to come for Leeds United: seeing a crucial game snatched away from them by refereeing that was idiosyncratic, or worse. The match against Chelsea became the first of a notorious collection engraved on the hearts of Leeds United supporters. At the interval,

Leeds were 1-0 down to a fine goal; a long, mazy dribble down the left wing by Charlie Cooke and a teasing cross which was finished by a flying, close range header from Tony Hateley. As Leeds besieged the Chelsea goal in the second half, Terry Cooper had a goal disallowed for offside and Paul Reaney a shot blocked on the line. Two minutes remained when Norman Hunter, advancing down the left, was fouled by Bobby Tambling. Referee Ken Burns awarded a free kick but became distracted by efforts to shoo back the Chelsea players ten yards. Johnny Giles waited briefly before rolling the ball a few yards square to Peter Lorimer, whose shot scorched past Peter Bonetti into the Chelsea net. Referee Burns was unready for the kick to be taken, he decreed no goal: the match and the Cup run ended amid uproar and a strong sense of grievance.

Less so Leeds United's assault on the Inter Cities Fairs Cup in 1966/67, which produced some stern encounters but nothing like the warfare of the previous season. DWS Amsterdam were no match in the second round – Leeds winning 8-2 on aggregate – but the third-round tie against Valencia, with whom Revie's men were uncomfortably familiar, was a much more searching test. Leeds' 3-1 aggregate victory included a 2-0 win in Spain, secured by goals from Giles and Lorimer, and hailed by Revie as one of their finest in Europe. It had been achieved despite disruptive injuries that forced the Leeds manager to field Jack Charlton at left-back and Billy Bremner as an unlikely centre-half.

The fourth-round matches against Bologna were tense, tight affairs which, while the Italians often had the upper hand, ended 1-1 on aggregate. Further progress for Leeds depended on the toss of a coin; for once Revie's men had luck when it mattered and in the semi-final were paired against Kilmarnock. The Scottish team never recovered from a 4-2 defeat in the first leg at Elland Road, remembered most for Rod Belfitt's hat-trick. Leeds' 0-0 draw in the away leg on 24 May gave them a passage to the final. Such were the last rites of a grinding season in which the team's reputation for being durable, discomfiting but unlovable opposition had been reinforced. Once more they were empty-handed but there was optimism too, for the chance of a European prize still lay over the horizon.

"We thought a lot about our game and picked up traits from the Continentals. What we called cynical in this country was called professional when the Italians played it. We picked it up from them how they would just walk out to take a corner, or feign injury if the game was getting a bit heated. Things like that."

Billy Bremner

The unrelenting pressure of playing for high stakes meant not only that Revie's young bloods were developing even greater reserves of physical and mental strength but were also becoming more sophisticated. Billy Bremner had become an established Scottish international; Norman Hunter had broken into the England team and would, in time, be joined by Paul Reaney, Terry Cooper and Paul Madeley; Gary Sprake and Johnny Giles were regulars in the Wales and Republic of Ireland sides respectively. Guile, craft, the capacity to strike fear into opponents: when Leeds achieved a harmonious balance of all these things, playing against them was, as numerous contemporary players put it, sheer murder. Leeds United's struggles and disappointments, Don Revie's iron-willed belief in the players' capabilities and a sense of paranoia deriving from the conviction that they were more sinned against than sinners bound the side tightly together. When things got rough, as often they did, Leeds United would close ranks, scrap, argue provocation, whatever it took to keep their end up. From turbulent expeditions abroad, they had learned some elements of gamesmanship.

Bremner reflected on those hectic days: "We thought a lot about our game and picked up traits from the Continentals. What we called cynical in this country was called professional when the Italians played it. We picked it up from them how they would just walk out to take a corner, or feign an injury if the game was getting a bit heated. Things like that." There were no stars; no individuals were allowed to behave like pop idols and upset the equilibrium at Elland Road. However strong-willed the likes of Bremner, Charlton and Giles were, Revie was wont to be ruthless with anyone who stepped out of line. The once shambolic club was now run like a crack regiment: short haircuts, club blazers, control of junior players' finances, sex education and lectures on etiquette were all part of the regime. It would not have suited every player; certainly not George Best of Manchester United.

Despite Revie's emollient public face, reserve wing-half Jimmy Lumsden knew Revie as a 'hard, hard man'. "His family had struggled and I think he thought: This will never happen to me. If you did something wrong, he would nail it right away. He sacked one of the younger lads for misbehaving while he was in digs on his own with the landlady away. But," says Lumsden, "Revie could also be kind and considerate. When my father died, he was fantastic. He spoke to me for an hour, told me to take as much time off work as I liked. He sent flowers down to my mother, then got her down for the week and paid for it. That's how he created the spirit at the club. He looked after people."

Meanwhile, it was with Manchester United, the reigning champions and widely portrayed as a collection of brilliant free spirits, that Revie's Leeds were unfavourably compared. Having built the team on the foundation of uncompromising defence, the Leeds manager was slow to see what players might do instinctively rather than with their minds cluttered with details from Syd Owen's dossiers and orders not to take risks. The 1967/68 season was scarcely into its stride before the final of the Inter Cities Fairs Cup, held over from last season, was upon his men. A home draw and two away defeats in the first three league games bode ill for the trip to Dynamo Zagreb on 30 August, as did injuries to Giles, Bell and Johanneson. Yet everything went according to plan for the first 40 minutes, with Leeds not only containing Zagreb's attack but carrying the more potent threat through well-controlled raids.

Having played like a team that had learned all its European lessons, the Leeds defence was suddenly wrong-footed by a raking right-wing cross that was headed home by the 18-year-old reserve Cercek. It signalled a rocky middle period of the game in which, on the hour, Revie's men succumbed to another move down the right. With Jack Charlton pulled out of

A genius at work: Billy Bremner's theatrical overhead kick is the final blow for Chelsea as they are demolished 7-0 at Elland Road in October 1967.

position as Zambata advanced, Rora seized on the swift centre and swept the ball into the net. Leeds' spirited quest for a late away goal came to nothing. Although two goals down, Revie was still preaching caution in his team talk before the second leg at Elland Road. Mike O'Grady, perhaps the most individualistic member of the team, recalls his frustration as Revie talked through opponents who were already familiar, warning him about the other winger. "You'd be sitting here thinking 'God, just let us play'," O'Grady said. Putting Paul Reaney on the right wing underlined how desperate the need had become for Leeds to find a genuine forward.

Leeds threw themselves forward with plenty of fervour but little imagination. Pumping forward aimless high balls was no way to pierce a ten man defence. Efforts from Charlton, Greenhoff, Belfitt and Bremner all went close but the match, which ended 0-0, was not one in which Leeds were robbed; rather one in which their inability to improvise was exposed.

With the fans' clamour for a striker intensifying, Revie finally acted. On 22 September 1967, he signed the young Sheffield United centre-forward Mick Jones for £100,000, much to the consternation of the Bramall Lane faithful. Although Jones, 22, had scored 63 goals in 149 league matches, he still had some way to go before becoming the finished article. But once his technique and fitness had been worked upon, Jones became a rock in attack, recklessly brave, a master of shielding the ball when closely marked, with a legendary willingness to chase any cause.

He made his début in the 3-2 home win against Leicester City on 23 September. Ronald O'Connor, writing in *The Daily Telegraph*, described Jones' arrival as appearing to make Leeds lightheaded: "They attacked with such careless abandon that their usually resolute defence quivered." Meanwhile, Jones distinguished himself by mastering Leicester's central defenders in the air. His was not a scoring début but then he rarely went in for theatrical performances. Running off the ball, launching himself into danger areas for the common good: these would become the Jones trademarks.

While there was no sign of lightheadedness in Leeds' next league fixture, a barren, error-strewn, 0-0 draw at West Ham, the following home performance, against Chelsea on 7 October, saw Revie's men play like a team that had been prescribed a strong tonic and taken triple the recommended dose. Three days earlier, the Leeds attack had tucked into the part-timers of Spora Luxembourg in a Fairs Cup first-round tie, and scored nine goals without reply. Chelsea, although near the relegation zone and managerless following the controversial departure of Tommy Docherty, were meant to be Leeds' equals. Yet Leeds set about them as if still playing the sacrificial Luxembourgers. It was a 7-0 rout with Bremner driving his side forward in energetic and inspirational manner before starting four weeks suspension. Goals came from all sides and angles: six Leeds players, Johanneson, Greenhoff, Charlton, Lorimer, Gray and Bremner scored. Leading by three goals after 14 minutes, Leeds played with flair, instinct, skill and without any let-up. Bremner crowned a mercurial display with the final goal, a superb overhead kick.

The first division learned something new about Leeds that afternoon: that Revie's side didn't need to be menacing; it could wreak havoc through skill alone. Yet despite having seen the evidence, Revie long remained fearful of lesser teams, seeking to shut them out rather than preaching that they should be carved open.

Through the autumn, Leeds made steady progress up the first division table, in the Inter Cities Fairs Cup and in the Football League Cup, a competition for which hitherto they had shown little aptitude or interest. Attendances at home games in the early rounds – 11,473 for the 3-1 win over Luton Town, 20,927 for the 3-0 victory against Bury – appeared to reflect the apathy of the crowd. Leeds had now worked up their familiar mid-term head of steam and after being comprehensively outplayed in a 2-0 defeat at Liverpool on 2 December, Revie's players hit their richest vein of form for three seasons in a mighty unbeaten run that would last until April.

The return of Giles, who had missed most of the first half of the season through injury, was an important factor. Although the team had also struggled through lacking Jones, who was

Opposite above. Running, always running. The burdens shouldered by centre-forward Mick Jones created countless opportunities for team-mates. Opposite below. The men who made Leeds United great. Don Revie (centre) is flanked (left to right) by youth team coach Cyril Partridge, physiotherapist Bob English, coach Syd Owen and trainer Les Cocker.

injured sporadically during his first two months at Leeds, Revie's team recorded some noble victories even when patched up with reserves or playing men out of position. Among these was the 2-1 win at Partizan Belgrade in round two of the Inter Cities Fairs Cup, achieved in the face of severe provocation and despite substitute Mick Bates being sent off for retaliation. It was unsurprising that Leeds had appeared jaded when playing Liverpool at Anfield three days later. Victories at Sunderland (2-0) and at home to Stoke (also 2-0) sustained Leeds' stealthy progress in the League Cup.

By mid-January, following successive 5-0 league victories against Fulham and Southampton – the latter a virtuoso performance of composure and control on a frozen pitch – Revie's men had clawed their way to second place in the table and reached the League Cup semi-final. They were to embark on another turbulent run in the FA Cup and remained hardy perennial competitors in the Fairs Cup, though made heavy weather of finishing off Partizan Belgrade (3-2 on aggregate) and Hibernian (2-1 on aggregate) to reach the fourth round.

Leeds' opponents in the League Cup semi-final were Derby County. Masters of two-legged battles, Revie's men knew too much for their second division opponents. At the Baseball Ground, they soaked up the home side's pressure before deflating them with Giles' 65th-minute penalty. At Elland Road, Derby took a surprise early lead but that only stung Leeds into going at them full blast. Losing 3-2 on the night to goals from Belfitt and Gray, Derby were overpowered by a team that was developing a lust for steamrollering the opposition.

Suddenly, Leeds faced the momentous prospect of a Wembley final against Arsenal. They had yet to master the big occasion; there had been few more stilted performances than that of Revie's men in the 1965 FA Cup Final and ever since, whether through nerves, fear, or some collective crisis of confidence, form seemed to desert them in crucial matches. Publicly, Revie denied that the team had failed him, repeating the line that his players had performed miracles in coming so far so quickly. Privately, he was desperate to win a trophy.

Saddled with this burden, Leeds United took the field against Arsenal on 2 March 1968, a day as grey and dreary as when they had faced Liverpool in their first Cup Final. It was a bad omen. Moreover, with Jones ineligible because he was cup-tied, Greenhoff struggling with a knee injury and Giles, Leeds' most creative midfielder, having recently suffered a bout of flu, the attack was severely weakened. However, there was plenty of muscle elsewhere and, long before its end, the match had degenerated into a dogfight. For all the abrasion of the contest, Leeds were the better footballing side. It befitted the nature of the game that the most stirring performances came from Cooper and Hunter who, in addition to soaking up Arsenal's obtuse pressure, enhanced the Leeds attack with forward runs.

A goal from Cooper after 17 minutes gave Leeds their first major trophy. An inswinging corner from the right by Eddie Gray, combined with Jack Charlton's awkward presence on the goal-line, had the Arsenal defence flapping. Cooper latched on to Peter Simpson's weak headed clearance and volleyed a left foot shot into the top of the net. It was the richest moment of an inglorious game. Having struck, Leeds retreated into their shell and the match sank into a contest of bestowing bumps and bruises.

How much were Revie's men to blame? No more, no less than Bertie Mee's Arsenal: on the day, these were two uncouth sides. Afterwards Revie said that he had wanted Leeds to play as attractively as anyone ". . . but under the circumstances, we would have been foolish to attempt this . . . we were playing with virtually nine fit men."

Revie's players knew how to dazzle when in the mood but had set their faces firmly against entertainment in the interests of victory. Leeds United had at last made an imprint on history. It seemed to matter above all else. Supporters, in much greater force than they had been for the FA Cup Final against Liverpool, roared Leeds on with a fervour that made clear they had shed their sense of being inferiors at the big occasion. No outsider could detract from their joy at the club's finest hour.

Leeds' form held for another five weeks before the weight of expectations and fixture overload began to take its toll. Meanwhile, they had edged past Hibernian in the third round of the Inter Cities Fairs Cup, winning 2-1 on aggregate and, in the fourth round, disposed of Glasgow Rangers with disciplined defence, counter-attack, and spells of unremitting pressure. Rangers' inability to make territorial advantage count in the 0-0 draw at Ibrox cost them dear midway through the first half of the second leg at Elland Road in which Leeds struck twice with goals from Giles (a penalty) and Lorimer.

As late as mid-April, Leeds United were sustaining a campaign on three fronts. Progress in the FA Cup had been a torrid saga of fierce battles and hard knocks: the fourth-round victory against Nottingham Forest (2-1), the fifth-round conquest of Bristol City (2-0) in which Gary Sprake was sent off, and the quarter-final clash with Sheffield United (1-0) were all hostile, unforgiving spectacles for the Elland Road crowd. As their semi-final encounter with Everton loomed, the first cracks appeared in Leeds United's form. By 12 April, Good Friday, Revie's team had played 55 matches when they came up against Tottenham Hotspur at White Hart Lane. Spurs, often accused of being insufficiently tough to overcome hustling combative sides such as Leeds, matched the Yorkshire team for effort throughout and surpassed them for skill. Two goals from Jimmy Greaves were decisive; Leeds' 2-1 defeat ended a run that had lasted 29 matches in all competitions.

It was not, yet, enough to bring the house down. Leeds' immediate response was to win their next three league matches: at Coventry (1-0); a turbulent and furious home encounter with Spurs (1-0) in which Tottenham striker Alan Gilzean was sent off and a disputed penalty by Peter Lorimer secured victory; then a less arduous 3-1 home win over West Bromwich Albion. Thirty-eight matches gone: four to go. On 23 April, the evening of their fixture at Stoke City, Leeds were one point behind leaders Manchester United with a game in hand. Ahead lay a semi-final tie in the Fairs Cup with Dundee; the FA Cup semi-final with Everton was four days away.

More punishment beckoned, more tension, with scant time to draw breath and regroup.

More was being asked of Revie's Leeds than any side in English history. Never had the pressure been greater not to err. Stoke City, a vulnerable side struggling to avoid relegation nevertheless contained skilful players who, when on form, could tear stout defences to pieces. Among these were midfielder George Eastham and striker Peter Dobing. Eastham's prompting and Dobing's inspired finishing unhinged the Leeds defence and, despite retrieving a two goal deficit, Leeds were eventually overrun. Dobing's decisive hat-trick left them facing Everton with their confidence sapped by a 3-2 defeat. They reverted to buffeting, safety-first tactics, combining aggression with dullness. A single disastrous moment three minutes before half-time undid them. Sprake, having earlier sustained a shoulder injury after falling when challenged by Joe Royle, found himself eyeball to eyeball with Royle once more after gathering the ball in the Leeds penalty area. Following a brief stand-off, Sprake's feeble kick went straight to Jimmy Husband. Husband's goal-bound chip was deliberately handled by Jack Charlton and Morrissey's penalty decided the game.

The fantasy of winning four trophies in a season was over and the match blighted Leeds' public image once more. Negative, unimaginative: again they were dogged by the old criticisms. Forgotten, it seemed, in any balanced appraisal of their season, were the bravura home performances against Chelsea and Southampton. Not that Revie's team had time to worry: the league, in theory, was still there to be won, the Fairs Cup clash with Dundee beckoned and, four days after the débâcle against Everton, Revie's men were much more positive as they secured a 1-1 draw from the first leg in Scotland. The 2-1 aggregate victory over Dundee would be Leeds' final crumb of comfort.

On 4 May, a week after the Everton defeat, Revie's ambitions of winning the league suffered a mortal blow as Liverpool came from behind with goals in the last six minutes to win 2-1 at Elland Road. This time Leeds were denied not by over-caution – it had been one of their brightest displays for a while – but by the indomitable spirit of opponents who, scenting frailty, pressed and pressed again until they found a way through.

Thereafter, Leeds could only pray for for failures by others. Meanwhile, Manchester City and Liverpool had muscled in among the contenders. Three days later, Leeds' hopes were finally torpedoed in a 4-3 defeat by Arsenal at Highbury. Manchester City, timing a late run of form to perfection, were to steal the crown. For Leeds, 1967/68 ended with a strong sense of more having been lost than won. Again there remained work to be done: once more fixture congestion had caused the Fairs Cup Final to encroach on a new season.

A study in concentration . . . yet for all his talent, lapses by Gary Sprake in key matches cost Leeds United dear.

While critics rationed praise for Leeds United's achievements, there was one matter on which they agreed: so strong was Revie's squad that whatever the disruption caused by injuries and suspensions, any side he chose to field would be a match for top-class opposition. Only at Burnley in the final league game of 1967/68, by way of experiment when all was lost, did Leeds field a team that wasn't up to the job. Of the five young reserves making a rare appearance in that 3-0 defeat – Nigel Davey, Bobby Sibbald, Jimmy Lumsden, Terry Yorath and David Harvey – only the latter two progressed to a career at the top level.

In all, Revie had used 25 players during the campaign. No-one played in every match, though Reaney and Hunter each missed only two league games. Occasional players such as Mick Bates, Rod Belfitt and Terry Hibbitt, none of whom ever commanded a regular first-team place, buttressed the side and kept things going smoothly. As long as Johnny Giles continued to flourish, opportunities for Bates, a neat, stylish player who favoured the left side of midfield, would be limited. Less creative and inspirational than his mentor, Bates nevertheless had the knack of slotting in as if he had played in the team all his life. Although content to remain on the fringe of things, he made 151 appearances in all competitions during ten seasons at Elland Road.

A more potent talent was left-winger Terry Hibbitt, whose misfortune was to be overshadowed by Eddie Gray. Hibbitt's carefree, irreverent disposition provided light relief at Elland Road and his sparkling skills illuminated some drab performances. He had a stronger sense of his own worth than did Mick Bates and, finding himself still in the shadows four seasons later, moved to Newcastle United where his talents matured handsomely. Hibbitt's untimely death from cancer at the age of 47 was mourned by supporters of both clubs.

Often Revie kept his regulars on the treadmill when they should have been resting. Billy Bremner, as tenacious as anyone, said: "Over the years, a good 70 per cent of the lads played in games where they shouldn't have done. I remember the Cup game against Sunderland (1966/67). I did my knee ligaments at Southampton the previous Saturday. Yet I was in the team. I couldn't believe it. On the morning of the game, Les Cocker gave me a fitness test and did a couple of block tackles that almost killed me. I said that there was no way I could play. But the boss said he'd rather have me with one leg than anyone else with two, to gee the other lads up."

However, Bremner was fit and raring to go when 1968/69 began with the unfinished business of the Inter Cities Fairs Cup. Leeds' opponents, Ferencvaros, were among the most accomplished teams in Europe. There was a curiously unseasonal feel to the first leg, played on 7 August when half of Leeds was on its summer holiday. This, combined with television coverage, reduced the crowd to a meagre 25,268. The match, frequently untidy, saw Leeds sucked forward by the Ferencvaros tactic of defence and quick counter-attack. Revie's men won through using familiar, if inelegant methods, Jack Charlton once more disrupting the best-laid defensive plans by standing on the goal-line as Lorimer swung in a corner, heading the ball down for Mick Jones to force home the only goal of the game.

It was a tenuous lead to take to Hungary for the second leg one month later. Ferencvaros, playing before 76,000 partisan fans and guided by the great Florian Albert, were a formidable force but anything they could do in terms of defending and relieving pressure by occasional upfield sorties, Leeds could surpass. Sprake, so often maligned, had a supreme night, an unbeatable last line of defence on the rare occasions that Ferencvaros pierced the Leeds

Above. Cheeky, skilful, though fated never quite to fit in. Terry Hibbitt was eclipsed by Eddie Gray while at Elland Road but his talent was fulfilled when he moved to Newcastle.

Opposite. First into the tackle. Jack Charlton showing his usual commitment against Crystal Palace.

rearguard. Other towering performances came from Madeley, Hunter and Cooper. Leeds' only attacking gesture of any menace was a header from Mick Jones that dropped on top of the Ferencvaros crossbar after he had risen to meet a free kick from Mike O'Grady. The Fairs Cup was hard-won and deserved.

This time, with the silverware came a better press. For a stonewall display of defensive football in foreign lands against illustrious opponents, Leeds' efforts were adjudged heroic. Yet such was their crowded calender, there was little time to savour the triumph. Within a week of winning the trophy on 11 September, Leeds had to start defending it, producing a stout-hearted, goalless performance against Standard Liège of Belgium in which Sprake was again outstanding.

Leeds embarked on their first division campaign with deadly serious intent, winning seven and drawing two of their first nine games: a run that might not have been foreseen when, in their opening match at Southampton, an own goal from Jack Charlton put them behind after 90 seconds. Yet several of those performances were unconvincing, impoverished because of the absence through injury of Johnny Giles, Revie's wiliest, most creative player. In recovering from their early aberration to win 3-1, Leeds' display at The Dell had hallmarks that came to epitomise their season. Richard Dodd, reporting for *The Yorkshire Post*, delighted in Hibbitt's contribution: "spindly-legged and more enthusiastic than anyone on the pitch . . . he scored with a brilliant left-foot shot for the third goal in 63 minutes." But, Dodd wondered, "was there any real need to slow the game down in the last 15 minutes in such a way that Leeds kept control at walking pace with casual and clever passes between three players, while opponents became frustrated with attempts to intercept?"

One great success of 1967/68 had been Terry Cooper who took over at left-back after Willie Bell transferred to Leicester City. With several players groping for form in the first two months of 1968/69, Cooper, Hibbitt and Mike O'Grady, with their irrepressible attacking instincts, provided most of the entertainment. Hibbitt, for whom no regular place could be found, did much to enliven Leeds in their second league match, a 4-1 win against newly-promoted Queen's Park Rangers that was much harder earned than the scoreline suggested.

Their third match was against Stoke City – described by Richard Ullyatt of *The Yorkshire Post* as the league's largest collection of elderly experienced gentlemen. However, this same collection of senior citizens had beaten Leeds 3-2 at the Victoria Ground four months earlier, puncturing Don Revie's hopes of taking the championship. In winning 2-0 with goals from Jones and Johanneson, Leeds profited when playing direct, thrusting football, yet frustrated supporters by dabbling in inconsequential passing routines across the pitch. The sternest early test came on 31 August with the visit of Liverpool, old adversaries against whom Leeds habitually came off second best. The game was an unedifying spectacle; defenders ruled, and everyone seemed intent on cancelling out danger rather than creativity. Revie had grown prickly about his critics in Fleet Street yet it was a Yorkshire reporter, rather than a London journalist disparaging the match from arm's length, who wrote that "of 12 players each side used, not one was more than efficient". Meanwhile, 30 miles down the road at Hillsborough, Sheffield Wednesday and Manchester United were staging what *The Yorkshire Post* described as "a game in ten thousand," an enthralling encounter won 5-4 by Wednesday that crackled with life and invention, the mistakes of which were fondly forgiven and eclipsed by "the sheer genius of Best, Law and Charlton".

Inevitably, the sterile fare at Elland Road drew invidious comparisons. Yet Leeds, not Sheffield Wednesday or Manchester United, were top of the league. One Liverpool error had cost Bill Shankly's team dear: Ron Yeats failed to control a long through ball from Bremner and Mick Jones pounced to score the only goal of the match.

The pecking order at the top of the first division was not one to gladden soccer romantics but, at various times early in the season, Leeds had lacked Giles, Madeley, Gray, Lorimer and Cooper. Mike O'Grady strove to pep up a languid attack: he shone in the 2-1 home victory against Wolves on 7 September. Victory came four minutes from time after

Leeds had been 1-0 down and two weeks later in the 2-0 home win against Arsenal, O'Grady scored with a firm header from Cooper's centre, perpetually hungry for the ball as he raided both flanks. A week later, away to the champions Manchester City, Leeds' unbeaten run of nine league matches came to an abrupt end. Revie's men, swept aside by City's surges of attacking football, lost 3-1. It could have been much worse: when the defence was sickly, all else seemed to fail and, significantly, some of Leeds' more ragged performances coincided with a rare loss of form by Norman Hunter.

Few teams recovered more quickly than Leeds. By early October, normal service was resumed: within four days, they had extracted two 1-0 victories with displays of defensive expertise from visits to Newcastle and then Sunderland. Having won nine, drawn two and lost only one of their first 12 league matches, the habit of caution and adopting an acerbic approach when under threat seemed engrained. The visit of West Ham United on 12 October, whose fluid football attracted many admirers, was eagerly awaited and drew 40,768 spectators, Elland Road's biggest crowd of the season. Save for Lorimer's blistering goal from 20 yards, the fruit of a touched-on Bremner free kick, the match, which Leeds won 2-0, was memorable mostly for malevolence amid which West Ham's Harry Redknapp was sent off.

Opposite. Unassuming yet able, and one of Leeds' most loyal servants . . . for most of his 12 years at Elland Road, Mick Bates settled for playing second fiddle to Johnny Giles. Left. Last-ditch defence: Paul Reaney, one of the finest full-backs of his generation and a rock on which Leeds' success was founded, heads clear. He was another veteran of more than 700 matches and twice capped by England.

Peter Lorimer, one of Revie's best acquisitions, whose pace, control and thunderous shot thrilled Leeds' supporters.

Paradoxically, Leeds United were top of the league yet out of sorts and still groping for rhythm. Who, or what, might prevent them carrying on in similar vein throughout the season? The following week gave comfort to those who hoped that Revie's side might be toppled. Whatever it was that laid them low intermittently, Leeds' tentative display as they stumbled to defeat 2-1 in a League Cup tie at Crystal Palace on 16 October, suggested that the malaise was still about them.

The visit to Burnley three days later confirmed that all was not well. Any hopes Revie held of his side easing back into form with a controlled performance were blown away as Burnley's exuberant young players tore into the Leeds defence, attacking with accuracy and speed. By contrast, Bremner and Giles appeared ponderous and were constantly dispossessed before they had time to set up attacking moves. Defenders, Cooper apart, were in a spin, unable to fend away the buzzing Burnley attacks that brought the home team a famous 5-1 victory.

It was a day that emphasised Leeds United's vulnerability and lack of cutting edge. While the defence pulled itself together almost immediately, the attack seemed to have run of ideas. The departure of Jimmy Greenhoff, sold to Birmingham City for £70,000, was felt more keenly than Don Revie might have anticipated. While O'Grady was playing with verve, too often Mick Jones toiled alone up front. Billy Bremner, however, saw the débâcle at Turf Moor as a fluke: "Everything Burnley tried came off – they would have beaten any side that day," he said.

After their embarrassment at Burnley, Leeds set about repairs as they always did: stabilising themselves at the back, ensuring safety first. The next three matches, 0-0 draws against West Bromwich Albion, Manchester United and Tottenham Hotspur, provided variable, though limited entertainment. Leeds' visit to Old Trafford proved that George Best, lauded as Britain's greatest footballer, was incapable of outwitting Paul Reaney, whatever sorcery he might attempt. "As usual, Best found himself playing rabbit to Reaney's stoat," reported *The Yorkshire Post*, with a hint of glee. Speed, durability, determination, hard tackling and a knack of making crucial goal-line clearances were the Leeds right-back's trademarks. Still only 23 when the season started, Reaney had matured into one of England's finest defenders.

Leeds had looked for a win at Old Trafford, pressing forward for much of the match. The draw against Spurs was technically absorbing rather than enthralling; Bremner and Giles poking about in vain for openings. At Coventry a week later, they found a way through at last, with a goal described by *The Times* as "clinical and precise as a surgeon's knife," Bremner's chip from the right being adroitly side-footed down by O'Grady and then struck home by Madeley.

The Coventry performance had been characterised by a display of perpetual energy from Bremner, now showing signs of bestriding the gap that separates the fine players from the great. Succeeding Jack Charlton as captain had helped him calm down: fiercely combative by nature, Bremner had long been susceptible to provocations, blatant and sly. Technically there was not a weakness in his game and, although only five feet five, he was a menace even in the air. Winning the battle with himself, quelling the urge to lash out, Bremner harnessed his potential which, when properly channelled, enabled him to plot the demise of the best teams in Europe.

Buoyed by the win at Coventry, Leeds were in good heart when, on 26 November, they took to the field against championship rivals Everton. The contenders produced a stirring contest in which Bremner, Giles and Madeley ultimately got the better of midfield combat against the Everton trio of Alan Ball, Howard Kendall and Colin Harvey. Terry Cooper, too, had a fine match but the decisive goal came when Jack Charlton, supporting Leeds' relentless second-half surge, embarked on a stumbling run from which the ball broke to Eddie Gray. Gray's accurate left-foot volley was decisive, the battle went to Leeds, 2-1.

An earnest campaign to win the league, thoroughly prepared and rigorously pursued, would have sufficed for most teams. Life was never so simple at Leeds; the workload always punishing. November's distraction was an Inter Cities Fairs Cup tie against the Italian team Napoli. If Don Revie had assumed that barbaric matches in Europe were a thing of the past, the away leg of the contest came as a rude awakening. Travelling to Italy with a 2-0 lead, Leeds were up against opponents hell-bent on retrieving the tie whatever the cost.

Throughout the 90 minutes, Leeds withstood as much physical violence as in any of their continental adventures. They lost 2-0 yet won through to the third round on the toss of a coin. Reflecting on the battering his men had endured, Don Revie wrote in the next club programme: "I hope I never have to take a team there again!" Such was the concern for his team's safety, Revie and the board of directors considered withdrawing from the competition. With Leeds' desire for the Inter Cities Fairs Cup blunted after victory against Ferencvaros, the last thing Revie wanted, while in hot pursuit of the League Championship, was for any key player to be crippled in some half-hearted continental jaunt. In the event, Leeds soldiered on, making short work of Hannover 96, their third-round opponents, whom they beat 7-2 on aggregate. Not until March, when they found Ujpest Dosza in resolute mood and were themselves out of sorts, did Leeds finally relinquish the trophy, losing 3-0 on aggregate. Few grieved.

An often brusque and sporadically exciting 1-1 draw at Chelsea on 30 November, the high drama of which was confined to the last four minutes when both goals were scored, indicated that Leeds were continuing to recover confidence away from home. If victories were rarely emphatic, the performances were becoming more assured. The home game against Sheffield Wednesday on 7 December, which marked the halfway point of the league season, saw Leeds in fine attacking form, fashioning many more openings than the 2-0 winning margin suggested. Lorimer scored both goals; his second a brilliant flashing shot from an acute angle. Although lacking forwards who scored regularly, Leeds' ability to conjure goals from nothing served them well. Lorimer could strike a ball with more venom, from unexpected quarters, than almost anyone; Bremner, when moved upfield as an auxiliary attacker, had a genius for conjuring goals out of thin air. On the rare occasions that Leeds scored in profusion, it tended to be a collective feast rather than one man's gluttony. When Burnley came to Elland Road on 21 December enfeebled by injuries, Lorimer, Bremner, Jones, Giles and Gray all tucked in, dispensing a 6-1 thrashing, an apposite revenge for the humiliation at Turf Moor.

After winning 2-1 at Elland Road against Newcastle on Boxing Day, Leeds had 37 points from 24 league matches. Liverpool, who had played two games more, had 39. The championship now looked like a two-horse race. Liverpool were living off the fruits of an abundant early autumn: between 7 September and 5 October, they recorded five straight victories, scoring 18 goals and conceding none. Leeds never managed a comparable flourish but Liverpool had also lost four matches to Leeds' two. Whatever they did, however hard Bill Shankly might train them and make them strong with propaganda, they were being stalked by rivals who were no less durable.

Unlike other seasons, Leeds enjoyed luck at crucial times in 1968/69. The home game against Manchester United on 11 January was slipping away as George Best appeared to score from a deflected, indirect free kick in the second half. Leeds had lost their grip and a half-time lead when Bobby Charlton equalised but the outcome owed much to referee Bill Gow's mistaken belief that Best's kick had not touched a Leeds player. The effort was disallowed and Leeds regrouped, stealing the match with a winner from Mike O'Grady 15 minutes from time. It was good fortune also to be knocked out of the FA Cup by Sheffield Wednesday on 8 January, losing the third-round replay at Elland Road 3-1 after a 1-1 draw at Hillsborough. This meant that for once, Leeds' season could not become overloaded; whatever lay in store for them, their strivings would not founder through physical and mental fatigue.

On 24 January, Leeds emerged, quite miraculously, from their visit to Queen's Park Rangers with two championship points. Rangers, bottom of the table, attacked with the frenzy of a team fighting for its life after Mick Jones had given Leeds a second-minute lead. Rarely had Sprake and the rest of his defence endured such a bombardment, never during the season were the points so hard won. QPR twice hit the bar, missed a penalty and

From the moment he made his debut as a seventeen year old, Billy Bremner made an indelible mark. Although he was not a Revie discovery, Bremner was to become the focal point of the manager's ambitions.

33

peppered the Leeds goal with shots, creating such waves that even Bremner and Charlton floundered amid the disarray. The habit of not losing now became the habit of winning. Victory at Loftus Road was the first of seven consecutive league successes. These were of uneven quality; a curiously slapdash performance in the next home match against Coventry was held together by Bremner who, in stirring form on a bleak, sodden afternoon, scored two stylish goals in a 3-0 win. On 12 February, with a snowstorm swirling around Elland Road, Revie's team showed a much surer collective touch in beating Ipswich Town 2-0. It was fitting reward for a fluid, open performance that they should oust Liverpool from the top of the first division.

The immovable object was becoming an irresistible force. The sequence of victories against Chelsea (home 1-0), Nottingham Forest (away 2-0), and Southampton (3-2) finished with a cadenza at Stoke City (5-1) in which the home side was outwitted, outfought, outrun and overwhelmed as Revie's men stormed their way through frail defensive lines like a Panzer division. Between times, Leeds had enacted the last rites of their Fairs Cup campaign, losing the second, bruising leg of their tie against Ujpest Dosza 2-0, and 3-0 on aggregate. A bout of flu had weakened the team that did battle in Hungary and for the game against Wolves on 29 March, Revie's men appeared less robust than usual but Leeds were able to live off their wits, achieving a goalless draw in a subdued match that nevertheless had its well-schemed moments. In another goalless draw at Sheffield Wednesday, on 1 April, Leeds were a striker short of translating superior attacking ability into goals but on song in all other departments-quicker on the ball, harder in the tackle.

Four days later, at home to Manchester City, Revie's men appeared shot through with anxiety, as if gripped by a fear that the knack of scoring had deserted them when it mattered most. The problem had persisted all season; the lack of another striker to feed off the turbulence created by Mick Jones' hard running. City played a calm, self-contained game but they were undone and Leeds delivered from their state of angst, when Cooper broke down the left and, from a ball that bobbled off City goalkeeper Joe Corrigan, Giles gratefully netted the rebound. A week later at Highbury and by now smitten with championship fever, Leeds' good luck held throughout a fiery match that maintained the pattern of fierce encounters involving Arsenal. Barely four minutes had passed before the Gunners' centre-forward Bobby Gould flicked out with his heel at Gary Sprake while challenging for the ball. Sprake responded by flooring Gould with a sharp left hook. For all Arsenal's entreaties, and evidence of his misdeed in the shape of the prostrate Gould, the Leeds goalkeeper was allowed to stay on the field. The game, played in bright sunshine on a hard, dry pitch and in a swirling wind, was presented to Leeds by two grotesque defensive errors, both by Arsenal centre-half Ian Ure. After 14 minutes, Ure was caught flat-footed and exposed by a long through ball from Mick Bates. Mick Jones galloped away from him and planted the ball firmly past Bob Wilson. Three minutes after Arsenal had drawn level with a goal on 34 minutes from George Graham, Leeds regained the lead when Giles intercepted Ure's misdirected back-pass almost on the goal-line and walked the ball into an unguarded net.

A less thorough team than Revie's might not have had such breaks. As ever, management homework had detected the opposition's flaws. It was known that Frank McLintock, recently converted to defence, tended to stray too far upfield leaving Ure without cover; and that a probing through ball could slice Arsenal open. From the Gunners' League Cup Final defeat against Swindon, Leeds knew also that Ure was prone to making a hash of back-passes when under pressure. With Giles breathing down his neck, it had been proved again. Arguably Leeds had gained their points less by luck – save for the good fortune that Sprake had not been sent off – than by applied intelligence. Near the end, Leeds played keep-ball in a way that infuriated the home fans and many neutrals but Revie would leave caring about his team's lack of charm for some other, less crucial occasion. Bremner considered that Leeds were great that day, considering the conditions: "We took the steam out of Arsenal by playing possession football."

With four games to go, Leeds could only throw the title away; if they kept winning, Liverpool could not overhaul them. Despite the tension, Revie's team played some fluid, rippling football in the home game against Leicester City on 19 April. A delicious goal sealed their 2-0 victory: a Giles run, a centre glided in by Reaney on the overlap, and a sharp header dispatched into the net by Eddie Gray. Leeds were almost there: the players still fit, morale high. Experience of retaining their nerve and composure whatever the storm served them well three days later against Everton, who had managed to keep Leeds and Liverpool in their sights and might yet be champions if both suffered a catastrophic loss of form. As Everton poured forward, roared on by a 59,000 crowd, Revie's men rebuffed everything and twice came close to breaking the deadlock with efforts by Peter Lorimer as they lifted the siege through sharp counter-attacks.

A 0-0 scoreline still left Liverpool's hopes alive. The arrangement of fixtures could have produced no more dramatic denouement than for Leeds to visit Anfield in their penultimate game. The only demand on Revie's men was that they should avoid defeat, at which they had become grand masters. Liverpool came at them in a frenzy, like red hammers beating against white rock. Anfield was a cauldron, a madhouse of noise. Possibly the young Liverpool striker Alun Evans was overprimed, unsteadied by the cacophony and the frantic drama when, from two prime scoring chances, he produced an indifferent header and then shot high and wide with an open goal before him. A scorching effort by Ian Callaghan was tipped over by Sprake at full stretch as the bombardment reached its climax but the Leeds defence, unbreached, was sufficiently composed and forceful to repel Liverpool back into midfield. Marvelling at the colossal nature of the struggle, Geoffrey Green wrote in *The Times*: "It was total entanglement of heart and body . . . between two sides as hard as a diamond but without that stone's brilliant flame." Leeds survived with distinction, magnificently. Nil-nil was good enough; the League Championship was theirs. Despite the impassioned bias of the Liverpool fans, once the game was up, they found it in their hearts to acclaim the new champions like heroes. For Revie, to be lauded thus by the fervent followers of his arch rivals was a moment of exquisite joy and satisfaction.

Poetry in motion: Mick Jones in an aerial duel with Frank McClintock.

"They say they [Leeds] relish hard work; that the expense of energy seems an eternal delight. But surely there must be a limit."

Geoffrey Green, The Times

There were no half measures about Leeds United and their achievements. They had won the championship with a record number of points (67), the fewest defeats in a 42-match season (2) and the lowest total of goals conceded (26). But in 1969/70, there would be no respite and no question of Revie's ambition having been sated. The FA Cup still eluded him and the European Cup was a new and tantalising prospect. Save for Jack Charlton, his team was still young. It was only ever likely to become stronger; an unnerving prospect for any opposition. Of course, Leeds had struggled for goals, only 66 were scored in the league campaign and, whatever the strengths of his squad, Revie knew that he needed reinforcements.

In the close season he acted, spending £165,000 and breaking the British transfer record to buy the Leicester City striker Allan Clarke. Clarke, 23 when he arrived at Elland Road, brought with him a prodigious talent and a modicum of cockiness. The latter was rapidly knocked out of him, the former exploited to brilliant effect. Revie had bought not just an opportunist but a complete footballer: Clarke had learned his trade in midfield and the arts of passing a ball from Johnny Haynes, his mentor during two seasons at Fulham. No tutor could have instilled in Clarke the gift of finding goals out of nothing, or retaining composure in so aloof a manner whatever the pandemonium surrounding him. That was a matter of temperament. Clarke came to be spoken of not so much as a finisher but as an executioner for, with his efficiency, critics perceived a chilliness, a disengaged aspect of character as he pounced on defensive frailties and mistakes without mercy.

The arrival of a proven striker had been expected at Elland Road but the departure of Mike O'Grady, Leeds' sharpest forward the previous season, surprised many. O'Grady's form had earned him a second England cap and he had no desire to move. Despite a troubled start to the new campaign caused by a carbuncle on his foot, O'Grady never fully understood why Revie should want rid of him. He sensed it was a matter of temperament and circumstances; Revie's favourites rarely included personalities with so marked a streak of individualism as had O'Grady. Moreover he was single – not part of a family set-up. After transferring to Wolves in September 1969, injury, of which O'Grady had been blessedly free during Leeds' championship year, plagued him once more. Bad luck and an ill-judged move caused a rapid decline in his career, dismaying the many who had cheered the winger's exuberant performances.

Years later, when reflecting on 1969/70, Don Revie claimed that the championship was no longer a priority, that Europe and the FA Cup were his priorities. As the season unfurled, evidence suggested otherwise: Leeds appeared as omnivorous as usual, and the incisiveness provided by Allan Clarke made them more formidably equipped than ever. Yet, save for the style of their opening day 3-1 victory at Tottenham and an emphatic 4-1 win at Nottingham Forest two matches later, Leeds searched in vain for some rhythm. By drawing 0-0 with Arsenal between times, they surpassed Burnley's record of 30 first division matches without defeat but Leeds' progress through the seven matches compressed into August was frequently inelegant. Two draws with Arsenal produced conflict rather than art; 1-1 draws at Elland Road against Newcastle and Burnley confirmed that the whole seemed less great than the sum of its parts.

The eagerness of others to dispossess them was apparent: Everton, Liverpool and promoted Derby all made flourishing starts. Leeds' match at Goodison on 30 August against the league leaders was the first heavyweight collision of the season. The outcome was determined by form: the pretenders were flowing better than the champions who, preoccupied by the need to mark Alan Ball, were turned inside out by the rushing incursions of Everton

A full-blooded confrontation between Allan Clarke and Arsenal's John Roberts

wingers Jimmy Husband and Johnny Morrissey. Joe Royle, feasting on the service, scored two goals in addition to Husband's opener after five minutes.

If Leeds, 3-0 down, had been overrun, they were not to be blown away. Clarke and Jones appeared shackled but Bremner, ever the man for an emergency, hurled himself forward to chest home a goal. When Cooper and Lorimer carved Everton open for Clarke to score the second and trigger a furious late rally, it was a reminder that Leeds were still made of stern stuff even if Everton's bravura first-half performance was just enough to end the champions' unbeaten run of 34 league matches.

Leeds won two, drew four and lost one of their first seven league games. More than a month later, in the home match against Stoke (won 2-1) and Crystal Palace away (1-1), came reports of stuttering form. Even without total conviction, Leeds had, since losing at Everton, progressed through September with a draw and three consecutive victories. By the end of October, the first division reverberated to the martial tread of Revie's men tramping inexorably towards the summit. They were starting to show their true colours, a combination of style and strength that made them almost irresistible. On 29 October, Nottingham Forest came to Elland Road and were thrashed 6-1 in a match that had critics singling out half-a-dozen Leeds players for their excellent performances. Ten days later, at home to Ipswich, Leeds disregarded difficulties caused by a pitch covered in surface water and, with Giles dictating events from kick-off and Jones giving a superb display of aerial striking power, won 4–0, playing majestically throughout.

The first round of the European Cup was an opportunity for target practice. Leeds created a competition record in beating the Norwegian part-timers Lyn Oslo 16-0 on aggregate but for Revie's men the serious business began with the second-round tie against Hungarian champions, Ferencvaros. Handsome victories against Nottingham Forest and Ipswich gave Leeds all the confidence they could have wanted and, on a glutinous pitch they tore into their old adversaries, cutting them to shreds with powerful, quick-passing football. Three-nil down after half an hour, Ferencvaros, fêted as one of Europe's most talented football teams, could live neither with the Leeds blitz, the rain, nor the Yorkshire mud in which both teams became bogged down as the match wore on. By then, the battle was over. Driven on by Bremner, Gray and Giles, Leeds routed their opponents with two goals from Mick Jones and one from Johnny Giles. Geoffrey Green of *The Times*, veteran of many a big European occasion, wrote: "Had I not seen it, I would not have believed a Ferencvaros side full of such talented players could have been so ground down." The team that a year earlier had attacked Leeds so furiously in striving to overturn a 1-0 deficit in the Inter Cities Fairs Cup Final caved in almost without a fight. The prospect of winning the Fairs Cup attracted 76,000 to the Nep stadium; witnessing Ferencvaros' demise in the European Cup drew just 5,400. Although 3-0 up, Leeds set about the match as if all depended on it, dominating almost throughout, winning 3-0 once more with Jones again scoring twice and Lorimer crashing home a third near fulltime.

At home, November brought games against old rivals Liverpool and Manchester City. In drawing 1-1 with Liverpool at Elland Road on 22 November, there was a rarity: Leeds, after taking an early lead from a Johnny Giles penalty, were almost overpowered. Gary Sprake fumbled a header from Ron Yeats to hand Liverpool an equaliser and, with Paul Madeley withdrawn into a more defensive role, Liverpool pressed and probed. Late on, Leeds missed the best chance to seal the game when Giles missed a second penalty after Bremner was fouled in the area. After mud at Elland Road there was a rock-hard surface at Maine Road the following week with Leeds, according to *The Times*, "wearing a look of serene composure". In an absorbing, fluid match, Madeley was the outstanding defensive and midfield player and Leeds gained their 2-1 victory through a goal by Mick Jones three minutes from time.

No more could be asked of Revie's men than to keep winning and chip away at Everton's lead. They did so: after Manchester City came successive home victories against Wolves (3–1), Sheffield Wednesday (2-0) and West Ham (4-1). The latter, achieved on 17 December, not only confirmed Leeds' sparkling form but ousted Everton from first place, albeit that their lead was fragile: Leeds had 38 points from 25 games, Everton 37 from 23.

There was a rude, rumbustious interruption of Leeds' winning sequence when they went down 2-1 at Newcastle on Boxing Day in a match of five bookings, much acrimony and complaints that the referee had lost control. It heightened the tension of the summit meeting with Everton the next day, a duel governed by taut nerves and hard tackling. Everton played a wild, occasionally ruthless game but Leeds imposed order by scoring twice before half-time. Both goals came from Mick Jones: the first exemplified his commitment to chase any cause; the second his mastery of the air. When Everton resorted to football rather than intimidation, they had their best spell, pulling a goal back through Alan Whittle. They fought to the last and three minutes from time Morrissey's shot on the run hit a post. A goal then would have tilted the delicate balance of the championship in their favour.

Chelsea were the other contenders. Unbeaten in the league at home, they looked solid, consistent and full of flair. Leeds travelled down to confront them on 10 January 1970. A crowd of 57,221 squeezed into Stamford Bridge, expectations primed. With their team 2-1 up at half-time and Allan Clarke carried off after being injured, victory beckoned; nothing in the air forecast that after the interval, Leeds would dismantle the Londoners and scatter them in all directions. As usual, Giles and Bremner led the uprising. Chelsea were robust, adroit opponents but where there was weakness, the Leeds midfield probed; where there were defensive gaps, these were unerringly found. Aided by a frail performance from reserve goalkeeper Tommy Hughes, Revie's men plundered four goals in 17 minutes of the second half on their way to a 5-2 victory. Here was notice for millions watching BBC's Match of the Day that Leeds were combining genius, ruthlessness and strength in ways rarely seen in domestic football. In time, Chelsea would exact their revenge but now the league was becoming a joust exclusively between Leeds and Everton.

The 3-1 home victory over Coventry on 17 January put Leeds back on top as Everton lost 2-1 at Southampton. Although of the following four games, Leeds drew three and won only one (Manchester United 2-2 away, Stoke City 1-1 away, West Bromwich Albion 5-1 home, Tottenham 1-1 away), Revie's men displayed, by turns, style, determination, coherence and a fluidity that marked them as the best team in England. It was hard to believe, as Don Revie claimed years later, that his defence of the league title was half-hearted but the FA Cup had never been to Elland Road; Revie had savoured the prize as a player with Manchester City in 1956 and he was desperate to win it as a manager. Leeds nearly fell at the outset; league form deserted them in the third-round tie against fourth division Swansea Town, who deftly protected a first-half 1-0 lead until centre-half Mel Nurse was sent off for fouling Allan Clarke. The final half hour was time enough to exploit gaps in the depleted Swansea line-up; Leeds squeezed through via a disputed penalty from Johnny Giles and Mick Jones' header from a Terry Cooper corner.

A benign draw in the fourth round took Revie's men to the home of Isthmian League amateurs Sutton United. Leeds fretted and fussed as if they were playing Real Madrid: Syd Owen and a London-based scout were dispatched to weigh them up. The dossiers appeared: there was a flurry of anxious communications between the two camps when Leeds officials realised Sutton were importing 600 extra seats from Surrey County Cricket Club. The Leeds camp feared that their players might be injured if they crashed into the improvised accommodation. On the day, Leeds turned their modest opponents inside out, scoring six goals without reply between the 15th and 75th minutes. While Sutton's centre-half John Faulkner marked Mick Jones so assiduously that Don Revie was moved to sign him, no-one policed Allan Clarke, who scored four. Leeds were magnanimous in victory; Sutton, who played some sweet football, were left to wonder what history might have been created had they converted the first clear opening of the match after ten minutes.

In the fifth round, Mansfield Town proved almost as stubborn as Swansea, and a 2-0 victory with goals from Clarke and Giles owed more to hard labour than excellence. In the sixth round at Swindon, Leeds snuffed out their optimistic second division opponents with

The versatile Paul Madeley who, in the 1966/67 season, appeared in every position except goal and inside-left.

two piercing first-half strikes from Allan Clarke, the second a masterpiece and the fruit of brilliant teamwork. Mud, the passion of a partisan Wiltshire crowd, unfamiliar surroundings: Leeds rode it all, bolting the defence after administering their lethal blows. They were, it seemed, a team for all seasons.

However, 1969/70 was not quite like other seasons. It had started early so that all business might be ended by April, allowing England adequate time to prepare their defence of the World Cup. As February gave way to March, Leeds' matches stacked up, each more oppressively important than the last. At stake was a fabulous treble: League Championship, FA Cup and European Cup, and there were no signs of them weakening. On 4 March, Leeds travelled to Belgium for their European Cup quarter-final tie against Belgian champions Standard Liège and displayed a classic talent for soaking up pressure then running a game to order. With 20 minutes remaining, Liège were undone by a rippling move that involved Madeley, the night's outstanding player, Giles and Cooper. Cooper's left-wing cross was gathered smartly by Peter Lorimer who bore down on the Liège goal and fired home from a narrow angle to give Leeds a 1-0 advantage.

If they could not win, Revie's men always did their damnedest to deny opponents victory. Usually they had the wit, will and stamina to succeed but now there was a torrent of big matches: after Liège on 4 March, they decamped to Anfield on 7 March for another taxing battle of guile and strength, another 0-0 draw into which both sides poured heart and soul, and claimed they had the chances to win. However satisfactory a goalless stalemate was at Anfield, it served Revie's men ill in their FA Cup semi-final battle at Hillsborough against Manchester United on 14 March. After drawing Manchester's sting for much of the match, Revie's men launched a ferocious assault on Alex Stepney's goal in the final half hour and would have much cause to rue his late, point-blank save from an Allan Clarke header near the end. Geoffrey Green, looking on for *The Times*, reflected: "They say they [Leeds] relish hard work; that the expense of energy seems an eternal delight. But surely there must be a limit."

On 18 March, in the second leg of their European Cup tie against Standard Liège, Leeds appeared uncharacteristically jittery. Although 1-0 down, the Belgians, who had already disposed of Real Madrid, had not abandoned the cause and almost levelled the aggregate score in the first minute, following a sharp raid down the right wing. As if disorientated by the swirling wind, Revie's men were often caught in possession and only began to impose their authority after the interval as Bremner stormed forward, urging his men on the offensive. The tie was settled 12 minutes from time when Lorimer was flattened in the Liège penalty area and Giles scored from the spot.

Victory appeared to be a source of infinitely renewable energy for Revie's men. Three days later, they were bouncy enough to take both league points at Wolverhampton Wanderers; goals from Mick Jones and Allan Clarke gave them a 2-1 win, although there was hardly time to count their knocks before travelling to Villa Park two days later for the FA Cup semi-final replay against Manchester United. On a night of torrential rain, Manchester came at Leeds like a whirlwind, as if sensing they must profit from playing against men with tiring minds and bodies. But trying to defeat Revie's men by fury alone proved fruitless. Once more the defence remained intact and with time came the familiar sight of Leeds emerging from cover and on to the offensive. Yet neither team cracked, not even in extra time.

The burden for Leeds of a second replay three days hence, with six more league matches and two European Cup semi-final matches against Celtic, all to be played inside a month, was becoming Herculean. No tyrant could have contrived a better plot to grind them down. Still they had not fallen. Terry Cooper, carried off with an injury at Villa Park, was back on parade three nights later for the second replay at Burnden Park, Bolton. From where could Leeds draw new inspiration? From Bremner, for one: hearing shortly before kick-off that he had been voted Footballer of the Year made him more buoyant than ever.

At last it was to be settled. After just nine minutes, though the tie had already run for 219, Leeds broke the deadlock. A chip from Peter Lorimer into Manchester territory, a leap from Allan Clarke, and the ball bounced off Mick Jones' legs to Bremner. One smart swing of the

*Opposite. Scenes from a momentous encounter. It took three battles to settle the 1970 FA Cup semi-final tie with Manchester United. George Best heads for goal but, as ever, there's no way past Paul Reaney and Jack Charlton. **Left.** Allan Clarke in full flight during Leeds' European Cup semi-final first leg against Celtic at Elland Road. But it was a match too far for Revie's men, now starting to show signs of fatigue as the big games piled up.*

Leeds captain's left foot, and the ball shot past Alex Stepney. What they had, they held for 80 minutes: neither through guile nor force could Manchester find a way through.

It was a joyous night. Yet, less than forty-eight hours afterwards, Leeds were forced to resume their pursuit of Everton with a home game against Southampton. The exhaustion and injuries sustained by key players could be concealed no longer: Bremner, Cooper, Reaney, Hunter, Giles and Jones were out of contention. There were no fitter, more willing players in England but Leeds were being asked to play, within eight days, four league games and the first of their matches against Celtic. The same men could not do it all. Already, the club doctor had identified five first-teamers as being mentally and physically fatigued. A flurry of bizarre happenings and absent-minded mistakes in the final twenty minutes of the home match against Southampton signalled the disintegration of Leeds' campaign. A goal on the hour from Peter Lorimer had given Revie's patched-up side the lead but ten minutes later began, according to Tom German of The Times, "a near fantasy . . . which could rival the most fanciful wit of Lewis Carroll". Jack Charlton, standing on the goal-line surrounded by a cluster of players, sliced the ball into his own net. Soon after, a harsh handball decision was given against Terry Hibbitt: Southampton scored from the penalty. When Terry Yorath mishooked a clearance into his own net, it concluded a miserable distortion of events. German had nothing but sympathy: "If they [Leeds] lose the championship, it is because of the commitments heaped on them by the rewards of their own talents."

Since Everton had beaten Chelsea at Goodison Park, Revie decided the game was up. On Easter Monday, he dispatched a team of reserves to face Derby County, two days before Leeds were due to face Celtic at Elland Road. Leeds lost 4-1 and the club was fined £5,000 by the Football League for deliberately fielding a weakened team. The Football League secretary Alan Hardaker was quite unsympathetic. In football matters, he considered Revie devious, selfish and ruthless, and had become impatient with his repeated requests for postponements of fixtures or for referees to be changed. Yet Jack Taylor, a leading referee of the era, took a kindlier view: "Revie looked at every angle. I don't blame him – he had a job to do. He was the ultimate tactician."

Certainly Revie was unrepentant. Two days later, all his crack troops save for Norman Hunter were up off their sick beds for the grand battle against Glasgow Celtic but they had been blunted by their colossal FA Cup encounters with Manchester United and were a yard slower than their fresher opponents, who had travelled down in high feather, backed by a huge body of raucous support. Leeds, strangely leaden and flat-footed, had no time to feel their way into the match before Celtic struck in the first minute. Centre-forward Willie Wallace controlled a high through ball then fed George Connelly who hammered in a shot that was deflected off Terry Cooper's leg past Sprake. Celtic were electrified: right-winger Jimmy Johnstone became a source of perpetual torment thereafter and Leeds never recovered from the shock. True, they had some bad luck: Eddie Gray's shot whipped through a ruck of players and rattled the crossbar, then Billy Bremner, the player whom Leeds could least afford to lose, was carried off with concussion. But for the first time all season, the players who had dispensed so many footballing lessons to their peers were outclassed.

It was symptomatic of Leeds' wretched fortune that, in the course of an inconsequential 2–2 draw at West Ham 24 hours later, Paul Reaney, one of Leeds' defensive rocks, broke his leg when accidentally colliding with West Ham debutant Keith Miller. Suddenly the season was taking on the complexion of a grand tragedy. The Times agreed, concluding that "the gods who watch over the brave were asleep last night, and while they nodded Leeds United suffered one more sickening blow". Still there was no respite: it was less than two full days before Leeds' youngsters took on Burnley at Elland Road. An otherwise meaningless 2-1 victory yielded a moment of fine art as Eddie Gray threaded an intricate pattern through and around a thicket of mesmerised Burnley defenders before planting the ball into the net.

Then came a lull from the bombardment, the luxury of seven days before the FA Cup Final without a match, so that Leeds might conduct their contest with Chelsea on an equal footing.

There would be no Reaney, of course – a grievous loss both for Leeds and England – but all the other regulars: Sprake, Madeley, Cooper, Bremner, Charlton, Hunter, Lorimer, Clarke, Jones, Giles and Gray, the most accomplished, battle-hardened football company anywhere, were fit to play.

The breather worked wonders. And how it was needed, for the heavily-sanded Wembley pitch was destined to make more than its usual strenuous demands on players. Less predictable was that the strange, stodgy surface would help dramatise one of the great Cup Finals. "It was," wrote Geoffrey Green, "not a classic but an epic . . . the finest final seen at Wembley since the war . . . that had everything from A to Z." Leeds took on the role of creative protagonists with Chelsea, more passive, still liable to uncoil like a startled snake and launch venomous counter-attacks. For the most part, Bremner and Giles ran the show in midfield and Gray, after an early bout of conceding possession, recovered to run rings around Chelsea right-back David Webb, leaving him as dizzy as if he had been pushed off a spinning roundabout. Leeds United were their old selves, full of power and vision. The show they put on was the essence of their season: hard-running efficiency marbled with grace yet undermined by ill-luck and lapses of concentration. The concoction of sand and mud confounded everyone's expectation of the bounce and played a role in the first goal: Jack Charlton's header failed to sit up as Chelsea goalkeeper Peter Bonetti had expected and dribbled across the Chelsea line.

It was 1-1 at half-time though, for Gary Sprake had absent-mindedly allowed Peter Houseman's long-range to squirm beneath him and into the net; but 2-1 to Leeds with four minutes to go. Perhaps Mick Jones' goal, struck with his left foot seven minutes from time after a header from Allan Clarke hit the bar, was too intoxicating, for Leeds, of all teams,

Scenes from the epic 1970 FA Cup Final. The Chelsea defence is deceived by the bounce as Jack Charlton heads Leeds into a 1-0 lead at Wembley.

dropped their guard a few minutes later, seemingly wrong-footed by a disputed free kick given against Jack Charlton. Over from the left came the ball and Ian Hutchinson sprang unattended into the air, his header leaving Gary Sprake stranded. Two bolts from The Blues put Leeds back where they started. Extra time was more a test of survival than a football match, and near the end played out almost in slow motion as players succumbed to exhaustion. Such inconclusive marathons had been the bane of Leeds United's season, though, once again, Revie's men had shaped soccer history: the result of their toil was to bring about the first Cup Final replay for 58 years.

There could have been no worse preparation for the trip to Glasgow four days later, where Leeds had to face Celtic at Hampden Park in the second leg of the European Cup semi-final. Since their swaggering triumph at Elland Road, Celtic too had had their morale dented, astounding almost all of Scotland by losing their Cup Final 3-1 to Aberdeen. The odds, though, remained against Revie's team. Their travails had been much more debilitating and it seemed certain that Celtic would be supercharged by the support of 136,000 supporters, the biggest crowd in European Cup history.

Leeds United, however, only gave up lost causes. Their experiences against Chelsea helped rekindle some self-belief. Celtic came like a hurricane for the first quarter of an hour but at the first sign of a respite, Leeds struck. Bremner collected the ball on the right from Norman Hunter, ran forward unchallenged and blasted a 25-yard shot into the roof of the Celtic net. Against the odds, Leeds had achieved parity. Celtic were quick to recover from the shock. The bombardment of Sprake's goal continued, the demonic twists and turns of Jimmy Johnstone bamboozled Terry Cooper and, though Leeds reached half-time 1-0 up, Mick Jones had become a casualty, taken off with a gashed leg.

Two minutes after the interval Celtic's long-threatened equaliser arrived as John Hughes steered a smart header past Gary Sprake. The cacophony with which it was saluted might have woken the dead. Celtic scarcely needed further priming; a few minutes later Hughes rampaged forward and, as Sprake launched himself forward to thwart another threat on his goal, a shattering collision left the Leeds goalkeeper prostrate, his leg too badly damaged to continue.

Out into the storm ventured David Harvey, whose talents in goal had been rewarded with a meagre ration of first-team appearances but this was not the night to make his name. Harvey's first touch of the ball was to retrieve it from the Leeds United net. Jimmy Johnstone, marauding forwards once more, set up Bobby Murdoch who lashed the ball past Harvey from just inside the penalty area. Leeds were down and out but capitulated bravely and with dignity.

Now there was only the FA Cup for which to strive. With two weeks recuperation before the replay against Chelsea at Old Trafford on 29 April, Leeds looked vigorous once more. Harvey, with Sprake still injured, retained his place in goal and Revie's men set about the match as they had done at Wembley, carrying the game to Chelsea. It was, reported Geoffrey Green, "a match of gleaming steel, mainly the broadsword, used with impunity by both sides . . . but one with vicious tackling – Boadicea might have been on parade." It took Leeds 35 minutes to carve a way through flailing legs and bared studs. Allan Clarke, surging through midfield, brushed past three Chelsea defenders and released the ball for Mick Jones who shrugged off two more players before hammering the ball past Peter Bonetti. It was a goal fit to win any Cup Final; notwithstanding the rasping challenges to which they were subjected, Leeds appeared to have a grip on the game but, with 20 minutes or so to go, Chelsea at last stirred themselves and began to wriggle free. "Osgood, Cooke and Hollins started playing beautifully; began to burn some magic fuels," wrote Geoffrey Green. Eight minutes later, the durable Londoners equalised with a goal of beauty and elegance that belied much of their earlier play. Charlie Cooke feinted and wove towards the Leeds penalty area before flighting a perfect ball to Peter Osgood who, lurking unmarked near Harvey's goal, sprang into the air and flashed his header into the net.

Opposite above. The winner – or so he thought. Allan Clarke hails Mick Jones' goal which restored Leeds' Cup Final lead with seven minutes to go. But Chelsea fought back to equalise.

Opposite below. Exhausted bodies and tired minds yet still more work to do: Don Revie exhorts his players to make one final effort before the start of extra time in the FA Cup Final replay at Old Trafford.

Three times Chelsea had hauled their way back when all seemed lost. Once more there was extra time; again Leeds drove forwards through the middle and down the flanks but, a minute before the interval, Chelsea delivered a fatal blow. Ian Hutchinson unleashed one of his destructive long throw-ins as Chelsea crowded the Leeds penalty area; John Dempsey's flick-on eluded Jack Charlton and at the far post David Webb, Eddie Gray's fall-guy for so much of the game at Wembley, nodded the ball home.

For the first time in a marathon that lasted 240 minutes, and of which 16 remained, Chelsea were in front. There was a dreadful inevitability about Leeds' failure, despite their frenzied efforts, to find a way back. They had, like Sisyphus, pushed three boulders almost to the top of three mountains only to see them back in the valley. Those who loved them now could only weep; most neutrals were touched by their fate. Brian Clough, in his role as television pundit before Leeds United and Revie were to incur his displeasure, told the nation: "They have made the season."

As his exhausted players sat in the dressing-room at Old Trafford, stupefied by the injustice of what had befallen them, Don Revie collected himself. "Forget this season . . . it cannot be revived. We've got to start all over again. We've done it before and we can do it now." Thus, through exhortations to future battles rather than the indulgence of self-pity, the Leeds manager sought to comfort his men. "Deep down in the heart of every Leeds player was a burning determination that never again would we suffer as we had suffered this season," said Norman Hunter. Defeated they were. But not broken.

"People didn't give us enough credit for picking it up every time. After what we'd been through, a lot of clubs, a lot of players would have collapsed. But there were never any public recriminations. Everyone kept quiet and we said we'd start again next year. We were the best team in the country."

Johnny Giles

Don Revie had assorted ways and means of keeping his side together. In a way, they thrived on momentous disappointments. "People didn't give us enough credit for picking it up every time," said Johnny Giles. "After what we'd been through, a lot of clubs, a lot of players would have collapsed. But there were never any public recriminations. Everyone kept quiet and we said we'd start again next year. We were the best team in the country."

The upright Syd Owen would succour the players simply by telling them they had done themselves justice. Revie, more practically, told his directors that if they wanted him to keep 16 or 17 good footballers happy, money must be made available for bonuses. Whether through fine words or the prospect of handsome payments, when Leeds United returned to start the 1970/71 campaign, scars had healed.

The same sturdy men, free from the cruel handicap of an overloaded fixture list, set about their rivals in familiar fashion. On opening day they outplayed Manchester United at Old Trafford, though Leeds' midfield superiority should have yielded more than the one goal – a thumping header from Mick Jones – that determined the game. Four days later at Tottenham, there was rarely any doubt about Leeds' 2-0 victory once a streaky, long-distance shot from Eddie Gray skittered past Pat Jennings, off the post and into the net shortly after half-time. Close season convalescence had done Revie's men the world of good.

These were the first of five successive victories, the hardest won of which was the third, at home to Everton, who twice led and shone brighter in a pulsating match before Bremner retrieved the match with two opportunist second-half goals. West Ham (3-0 at home) and Burnley away (also 3-0) provided less taxing opposition. Arsenal, in a goalless draw at Highbury, were the first to deny Leeds maximum points in a bruising rough and tumble. There was a sense of déjà vu about the controversies: the fury when Eddie Kelly was sent off for fouling Billy Bremner; the referee needing a police escort at full-time.

Leeds had been on their impeccable best behaviour at Manchester United yet rarely shirked from mixing it in the face of provocation, real or imaginary. They had taken an early casualty: without Giles, injured at West Ham, their midfield looked impoverished. Though four days later a 1-0 victory over Chelsea was a small measure of revenge for the events of April, it was poorer for the absence of Leeds' most ingenious creator. A week later, still lacking Giles and also Charlton, Leeds were off colour and overrun 3-0 at Stoke City, who were always liable to humble the best when in the mood. It brought the wave of teams below lapping a little closer but although Leeds' form stuttered for the next six weeks or so, the results held up: Revie's men embarked on an unbeaten league run of 17 matches, and were not overturned until 9 January when Tottenham won unexpectedly at Elland Road.

Undoubtedly their rhythm was interrupted by further injuries to Johnny Giles, who suffered a fractured cheekbone in the 0-0 draw at Nottingham Forest on 26 September that forced him to miss a further four matches, and to Eddie Gray, who became a long-term casualty after pulling a muscle during Leeds' 2-0 home victory over Huddersfield Town the following Saturday and then, later in the season, broke an ankle. The away game at West Bromwich on 12 October brought the welcome return of Paul Reaney who, noted Derek Wild of *The Daily Telegraph*, "had recovered so well it did not look as if he'd ever been out of the Leeds side." Seventeen minutes into the match and he was doing his party piece once more, showing perfect positional sense by heading a point-blank shot from Asa Hartford off the line with Sprake hopelessly beaten. In a 2-2 draw of rich entertainment, Leeds led twice yet incited West Bromwich to play their best football of the season.

A furious contest. Arsenal's John Radford moves in for the kill as Arsenal come to Elland Road in April 1971, seeking the League and FA Cup double.

The following week, amid incidents of virtuosity and violence, Leeds let slip a 2-0 lead over Manchester United, allowing victory to dribble away despite dominating most of the game. Without Giles, Jones and Gray, Terry Cooper had been their most potent attacker, causing turmoil on the Manchester right flank with his twisting runs. In the last half hour, the visitors plucked two goals out of nothing; the second from Bobby Charlton five minutes from time meant that Manchester became the first team to extract a league point from Elland Road.

Cooper's sparky talents were evident the following week as Leeds exerted complete control at Derby, winning 2-0, still a little off-key but with enough good habits etched into them to do the most effective things. The assured form of Nigel Davey, standing in at right-back for Reaney who, despite his fine show at West Bromwich was still not fully fit, also caught the eye. There was not yet great unease about the odd points that Leeds were dropping but few were rued more than that lost in the 1-1 draw at Crystal Palace on 7 November. Rarely had Leeds been more securely in control of a match after Peter Lorimer's goal gave them the lead early in the second half. Just three minutes remained when John Sewell, the Crystal Palace right-back and captain, lofted an airy ball towards Sprake that sailed through the Leeds goalkeeper's hands and into the net. If a Red Cross parcel had been parachuted through the November gloom, it could hardly have come as a greater surprise to Palace.

For Sprake, the blunder was another in his portfolio of infamous aberrations. But it did not upset Leeds' equilibrium. Immediately afterwards they recorded home victories over Blackpool (3-1), Stoke (4-1), an away win at Wolves (3-2) and then at home to Manchester City (1-0). At Wolves, they were poised, smooth and sharp, too clever, too knowing for stout-hearted, aggressive opponents. Against Manchester City, *Sunday Times* reporter James Wilson noted: "There was present . . . the touch of inspiration which turns a good team into a great one. Leeds normally field seven or eight brilliant players, and their whole squad does not include a weak performer. Quality and ability are at the root of their consistency." A single goal on 55 minutes from Allan Clarke settled a magnificent match.

Twenty games gone and Leeds had 33 points, four more than Arsenal, though the Gunners had a game in hand. Leeds' manner, imperious, artistic, efficient or ruthless when needed, gave them the air of champions. The following week they prised a point from Liverpool at Anfield by playing keep-ball after John Toshack had equalised Madeley's majestic headed goal within two minutes. Against Everton, fallen champions and skulking in mid-table, Leeds were too clever, too determined: one headed goal from Jack Charlton knocked them out and, for all their toil and early fury, Everton fashioned only two clear-cut chances. In the Inter Cities Fairs Cup, Leeds went about matters as seriously as ever. There was the usual mixed bag of opposition: first, the Norwegian amateurs Sarpsborg, beaten 6-0 on aggregate and then the dogged East German side Dynamo Dresden, whom Leeds beat only on away goals (2-2 on aggregate) following a grimly strenuous second leg in which Mick Bates and the German substitute Geyer were sent off eight minutes from time. The Czechoslovakian side Sparta Prague visited Elland Road for the third-round first leg on 9 December. The tie was dead by half-time: Leeds plundered the frail Sparta defence scoring five goals, and made it 6-0 by full-time, with another dozen or so near misses. The return leg was a formality, with Leeds, fêted like visiting potentates, steaming to a 3-0 lead before Sparta recovered some dignity with two second-half goals.

As the FA Cup trail began, memories of Leeds' everlasting trials of strength previous season were all but forgotten. Who could resist the lure of the nation's favourite knockout trophy? Revie's men least of all: they had yet to get their hands on it. As in 1969/70, the third-round opposition was modest, though a tie at Rotherham was a potential source of humiliation. With Bremner injured in the first minute and sharp tackling from the home side chopping up their normal rhythm, the Leeds team settled for a goalless draw. In the replay, fortunes swung and Leeds had to retrieve a 2-1 half-time deficit to gain their 3-2 victory.

The fourth round brought Swindon Town to Elland Road. Any illusions of revenge the

Wiltshire team may have nurtured for last season's quarter-final defeat were brusquely shattered. "Their challenge," reported Richard Bott in the *Sunday Express*, "was disposed of by Leeds with the nonchalance of a traveller depositing a paper towel in its receptacle after a wash and brush up." Swindon were crushed by a hat-trick from Mick Jones and a further goal from Allan Clarke.

When in the fifth round Leeds were drawn away to Colchester, languishing in the lower reaches of the fourth division, it must have appeared to Revie's men as if some benevolent force was at work with the aim of smoothing their passage to Wembley. Agreeable memories of the previous season's jaunt to Sutton, in which Leeds had conducted themselves like regal visitors to an outlying colony, were rekindled. So much for those who thought taking on Colchester would be gentle exercise in the Essex sunshine. All Leeds' knowhow, organisation and experience appeared to have been mislaid on the journey down the A1. The defence was all jitters, the midfield, without Bremner, hustled into disarray. Colchester chased, tackled, harried and, on 18 minutes, went 1-0 up as Sprake failed to cut out a lofted free kick, allowing veteran centre-forward Ray Crawford, who had long been the bane of Jack Charlton, to head home. Ten minutes later, Crawford made hay again, coming off the better when challenging Reaney for a high ball. Although both came down in a heap, Crawford was quicker to recover as the ball ran loose, his ball striking Sprake and rolling in off the post. Two-nil down at half-time: 3-0 after 54 minutes. A high ball lofted towards Sprake's goal eluded the Leeds keeper when under pressure from Dave Simmons, who leaped above him to nod the ball into the net.

That chaotic, triumphant goal completed the most sensational upset in Cup football since the Second World War. It was not quite that neat and tidy. Hunter and Giles sought to grab the game by the scruff of the neck, and each scored as Leeds belatedly snarled into action. By full time, Colchester were almost on their knees but three goals were one too many to overturn.

Leeds United were nothing if not thick-skinned. Back among their peers, away from the cramped confines of the tiny Layer Road pitch, they resumed normal service. A week later, Wolves were the visitors to Elland Road, sprightly opponents as ever yet Leeds, after a tentative first few minutes, took command, created four chances for each one made by their opponents and cruised to a 3-0 victory with goals from Madeley, Clarke and a Giles penalty.

The early stages of the game at Ipswich three days later suggested that Leeds were going to crash heavily; as if whatever bug had upset them at Colchester had become airborne and spread across East Anglia to the nearest first division ground. With Billy Bremner injured almost at the start, Revie's men found themselves 2-0 down after 25 minutes, just as at Colchester, the home crowd mocking their discomfiture. However, there was to be no repeat of the FA Cup calamity: three minutes later Allan Clarke pulled a goal back, the springboard for a second-half onslaught during which Leeds scored three times in the first 15 minutes, and went on to win 4-2.

After 34 matches they were still in command of the League Championship race, six points ahead of Arsenal, although the Gunners had two games in hand. At Chelsea on 27 March, Leeds suffered the setback of a 3-1 defeat at Chelsea, but recovered the following week to feast on Burnley's frailties and win 4-0, all the goals scored by Allan Clarke. Of Clarke's style, Arthur Hopcraft wrote in *The Observer*: "He accepts possibilities and alternatives with exceptional speed, and yet has such control that he never looks hurried when he exploits them. Only the frantic behaviour of opposing players around him reveals how sudden and punishing much of his work is."

So dogged, so unrelenting was Arsenal's pursuit that only a constant run of victories would suffice to fend them off. Each point chiselled away by opponents who were usually spurred into giving their all against Revie's men suddenly became of immense value to the Gunners. From highly-charged games at Newcastle and Huddersfield, Leeds managed only two draws, and went into their home game against West Bromwich Albion on 17 April four points ahead but with Arsenal having three games in hand.

Bremner taking control against Stoke City.

West Bromwich, without an away win for 16 months, might have been easy fodder had Leeds not been in one of their jumpy, out-of-sorts moods. Bremner and Gray, both of whom had missed most of Leeds' action since January, were still not match fit and the midfield appeared ponderous, lacking the wit to spring Albion's stifling offside trap. An error by Jack Charlton helped present West Bromwich with a 19th-minute lead when, under no pressure, he passed straight to Jeff Astle's feet. Albion swept forward unopposed and Tony Brown slotted the ball past Sprake. They displayed a tenacity and liveliness that Leeds found hard to subdue. A second goal, with Leeds so off-colour, was liable to be fatal. It arrived in circumstances that brought the house down: rarely, if ever, had the refereeing appeared so perverse; never had an English ground witnessed so furious a display of indignation from a crowd goaded beyond endurance. The infamy lives on whenever the incident is re-run on television. With all the Leeds players up in attack, Colin Suggett was flagged offside as a long ball came up from behind and was picked up by Tony Brown. Referee Ray Tinkler, 20 yards behind play, overruled linesman Bill Troupe and waved play on. Brown, almost with a sense of embarrassment, galloped on before squaring the ball to Astle, who was also offside as he knocked the ball into the Leeds net. As Bremner and company besieged referee Tinkler, on to the pitch ran 30 or 40 spectators, few of them habitual troublemakers. This was disorder born of true anger and uncontainable frustration.

Opposite. The goal that caused a riot. Leeds players are flat-footed as West Bromwich get the benefit of an offside decision and score, sabotaging Revie's hopes of winning the League Championship.
Below. Uproar at Elland Road. Spectators invade the pitch and referee Ray Tinkler is besieged by furious Leeds players as he allows Jeff Astle's 'offside' goal to stand. Albion won the match 2-1 and dealt a blow to Leeds' hopes of winning the 1970/71 League Championship.

What of the uproar? Barry Davies, commentating on BBC's Match of the Day proclaimed: "Leeds are going mad, and they have every right to." His indignation was spontaneously expressed, though not condoning hooliganism. The bitterness etched into Revie's face as he stalked off the pitch, head shaking in despair, is an abiding image. "Tinkler ruined nine months of hard work. At 1-0 down, Leeds were fighting back and Albion starting to crack," he said.

Arsenal cashed in, winning two games in hand and ousting Leeds from the top of the table for the first time, on goal average. Their long march was perfectly timed: they had five matches left and Leeds only three; though each had to play the other at Elland Road on 26 April. Leeds' victory at Southampton two days beforehand was to keep the confrontation alive. Aided by a bizarre own goal from Saints' defender Dennis Hollywood – grounds, perhaps, for believing that the whole world was not conspiring against them after all – Revie's men won 3-0.

Elland Road was filled to its 48,000 capacity long before kick-off for the visit of Arsenal. Spectators perched on the roof of the south stand, others clung precariously to branches of trees outside the stadium. Leeds played with the urgency of men who knew that they must win or else concede the championship. A pattern was soon established: Leeds would press and Arsenal riposte with sharp counter-attacks. Durable though the Arsenal rearguard was, it was unused to the saturation bombing Leeds inflicted on it in the second half. Three times defenders had to clear off the line. A minute from time, the deadlock was broken. As Allan Clarke stabbed a shot towards Bob Wilson's goal, Jack Charlton closed in a yard ahead of the Arsenal keeper, rolling the ball against the post only for it to rebound off a defender into the net.

Pandemonium ensued: amid wild celebrations, the Arsenal team pleaded for offside so vehemently that the game was held up for five minutes and police were at full stretch repelling would-be pitch invaders. With a game to go, Leeds had reclaimed top spot.

Against Nottingham Forest, they went out like champions, the midfield fizzing with energy and invention with Giles, Bremner and Gray back to their best. First-half goals from Bremner

and Lorimer barely reflected their superiority and Jim Barron in the Forest goal produced heroics, mixing fine saves with others he knew little about. "Leeds are a great team – let there be no doubt," wrote James Wilson of *The Sunday Times*. "If, however, they have a weakness, it may lie in the complex paths of the mind, rather than in any lack of football skills." Perhaps their apparent tendency to brood, to be over-anxious, and to be absent-minded at critical times deprived them of a championship which, with 64 points, they would have been sure to win in any other season. Wilson suggested that "the effects of excessive professionalism could be seen in an obsessional search for playing perfection, causing woods to be missed through an undue interest in individual trees". Meanwhile, Arsenal's inexorable march to the title had been interrupted only at Elland Road, their 1-0 defeat forcing them to seek a win at Tottenham if they were to clinch the title. Victory arrived in the style that became a motif for Arsenal's season, from a single goal ten minutes from time.

If there was not quite the savage sense of loss among Leeds supporters as felt the previous season, perhaps it was because some souls were building up an immunity; that never again could defeat be so crushing as it had been in 1969/70. Moreover, Leeds had kept going in the Inter Cities Fairs Cup, disposing of the Portuguese team Vitoria Setubal 3-2 on aggregate after a closely contested quarter-final. Drawing Liverpool in the semi-final revived the Leeds public's appetite for a competition about which they had become blasé.

The two games were as taut as any the sides had contested but a solitary headed goal by Bremner, playing up front after being restored to the side following injury, was enough to see Leeds through over two legs. Doughty defence and the failure of Liverpool forwards to keep a clear head when gaps arose, did the rest.

The Fairs Cup Final against the Italian side Juventus saw Leeds' season stretch through May to the beginning of June. The first leg had to be replayed after torrential rain in Turin turned the pitch at the Stadio Communale into a swamp, forcing abandonment of the game after 51 minutes. When the players resumed 48 hours later, they produced a classic match, fluid, combative and stylish which Leeds twice retrieved having gone 1-0 and then 2-1 down.

Opposite. *Some Arsenal fans cannot contain their frustration as Jack Charlton scores a controversial last-minute winner.*
Left. *Mick Jones shows his usual determination under pressure from a Juventus defender in the Fairs Cup Final second leg at Elland Road in June 1971.*

Their first goal came from Madeley's spectacular 25-yard shot after he had been fed by Peter Lorimer, the second from substitute Mick Bates with his first kick of the game. Terry Cooper overlapped on the left and his cross was mishandled by goalkeeper Piloni. Bates eagerly rammed the ball in from close range. For the Leeds midfield understudy, this was his finest hour.

The second leg at Elland Road, a stern, confrontational affair, nevertheless still crackled with good football. Clarke's 11th-minute goal, a superb snapshot on the turn, gave Leeds an early lead but was wiped out only six minutes later when Madeley gave away possession in midfield. Furino latched on to the ball passing to Anastasi – then, at £440,000, the world's most expensive footballer – who neatly slotted the ball past the advancing Sprake. Juventus, still capable of administering a lethal sting, continued to press, probe and raid. Terry Cooper did most to relieve the pressure, making sharp retaliatory incursions down the left and causing panic in the heart of the Juventus defence. In the end, the two goals in Turin were enough: once more the away goals rule had served Leeds nicely, allowing them to savour the half-forgotten pleasure of having a trophy to clasp, one that had been won with honour. Soon they would be roaring back in search of more.

Right. A taste of things to come? The programme cover for Leeds' Inter Cities Fairs Cup Final tie against Juventus celebrates the heroic victory against Ferencvaros in 1968.

Opposite. A rich consolation for Leeds: pipped by Arsenal in the 1971 League Championship race, they were not to be denied in the Fairs Cup. Bremner, in Juventus shirt, shows off the trophy.

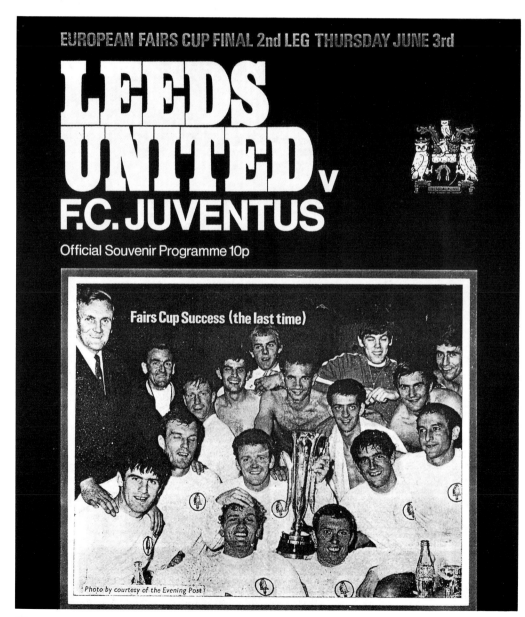

EUROPEAN FAIRS CUP FINAL 2nd LEG THURSDAY JUNE 3rd

LEEDS UNITED v F.C. JUVENTUS

Official Souvenir Programme 10p

Fairs Cup Success (the last time)

Photo by courtesy of the Evening Post

> *"I want Leeds to be able to match them on all counts;*
> *to have won everything in sight; to be a magnetic drawing card wherever we play . . .*
> *in fact I want us to be better than anyone else."*
>
> Don Revie

There was usually a hangover of some kind from one to the next of Leeds United's seasons. After the hullabaloo at the home game against West Bromwich which was compounded by scathing remarks made by Don Revie about the role of referee Tinkler, an FA disciplinary commission fined the club £500 and shut down Elland Road for the first three weeks of the season. Revie's men became nomads, setting up temporary camp at Huddersfield, Hull and Hillsborough, thence to Huddersfield once more before celebrating return from exile with a 1-0 win at Elland Road against Liverpool on 18 September.

For the first two months of the season, their form was patchy. Against Wolves at Huddersfield, Leeds' display in a 0-0 draw was dull and pedestrian; then they sparkled, as did Tottenham, in the 1-1 draw at Hull; they were rampantly destructive of Newcastle in the 5-1 win at Hillsborough yet somewhat laborious in beating Crystal Palace 2-0 back at Huddersfield.

Away matches, rather than the pseudo-home games, were the problem. By 9 October, Leeds had lost four – at Sheffield United 3-0, Arsenal 2-0, Huddersfield 2-1 and Coventry 3-1 – twice as many as in the entire 1970/71 campaign. It was hard to identify a single cause for the malaise. Key players suffered an assortment of niggling injuries and others appeared out of sorts at different times, Jack Charlton more often than most. Whatever, after 9 October with 12 matches gone – more than a quarter of the season – Leeds were slumming it in eighth position with only 13 points from 12 games, six fewer than the leaders Manchester United. They had also been swiftly deposed as Fairs Cup holders (the competition was now to be known as the UEFA Cup) by the Belgian team SK Lierse. Holding a two-goal lead from the away leg, Revie picked an inexperienced side for the return at Elland Road that suggested indifference to the outcome. Hardly a punter in the land would have put money on them losing 4-0 but there were few recriminations, more a sense of relief that the season would not become complicated by a tournament that had lost much of its allure.

In defeat at Coventry, Leeds looked lacklustre, ragged, and inhibited. A week later they perked up, beating Manchester City 3-0 at Elland Road then Everton 3-2 the following Saturday. Thus fortified, they travelled to Old Trafford for a battle with Manchester United who, a third of the season gone, sat comfortably atop the first division having taken 23 from a possible 28 points, four ahead of Derby County in second place. "Mature, purposeful professionalism is still able to overcome virtuosity of the highest order," wrote Rob Hughes in *The Sunday Times*. That day, Leeds were having none of Manchester's alleged virtuosity and squatted firmly on the likes of Best, Law and Charlton. Their own strike force of Allan Clarke and Mick Jones may have been absent, injured but Peter Lorimer was as eager and able as ever. His 30-yard strike on four minutes settled a game of high tension and no little violence. In dishing out the latter, Manchester United were quite the equal of Revie's men.

It was the Manchester United of old, whose flamboyant deeds made them national favourites, that Revie sought to emulate. "I want Leeds to be able to match them on all counts; to have won everything in sight; to be a magnetic drawing card wherever we play . . . in fact I want us to be better than anyone else," he said. It was the visionary stirring in him. Defend; fight; conquer the world in time; be remembered for greatness. Such was his long-term ambition.

Despite their triumph at Old Trafford, Leeds had not quite found top gear. Revie, feeling that they needed extra energy in midfield, moved to sign 21-year-old Asa Hartford from West Bromwich Albion. Hartford was a speedy, creative and ebullient player, who nevertheless might have been hard to accommodate when all the old troopers were fit. But after a fee of £177,000 was agreed, the transfer foundered when a medical examination revealed that

Mick Jones escapes the attentions of Tottenham's Phil Beal. Leeds won 2-1 and produced a performance that critics rated the best they had ever seen by any English team.

Hartford had a heart defect. It was enough to dissuade Revie from going ahead yet not to prevent the young Scot from fulfilling his promise with Albion and later Manchester City.

Although succumbing to a last minute goal at Southampton on 13 November and losing 2–1 in a match they had dominated throughout, Leeds' wobbles were becoming fewer. It was rare for them not to gather momentum in mid-season and, as key players slotted back into the side, even on off-days, such as in the rasping 0-0 draw at Chelsea on 11 December and 1–1 at Crystal Palace the following week, they were extracting a point each time for their exertions.

At home, Revie's men had once more started to appear invincible. By Christmas, they had forced their way up to fourth place, having taken 22 points from 29 games, five fewer than Manchester United. On 27 December, championship rivals Derby County visited Elland Road and were given the full works by a Leeds team that seemed to have rediscovered itself. Clarke, Jones, Lorimer and Gray created disarray, Bremner and Giles out-thought and outran Gemmill and McGovern in midfield; Hunter, Charlton and Reaney could not be prised open. The last of Leeds' three goals exemplified their exuberance: Clarke sweeping in from the left, providing Lorimer with the chance to thunder in a shot from 20 yards.

Liverpool, hosts to Revie's men on New Year's Day, were unbeaten at home in the league since March 1970. Leeds were unimpressed. They were in perfect harmony once more; a team for all occasions. With Liverpool generating more heat than light in the first half, Leeds cooled things down with a defensive display of great composure. In the second half they countered: Liverpool were carved open by the ingenuity of Giles though it was Clarke, then Jones, delivering a sucker punch ten minutes from time, who struck the two decisive goals.

With Leeds in such prime form and unencumbered by European commitments, the FA Cup looked full of promise. Although lacking Jones, Clarke and Charlton, they made short work of Bristol Rovers in round three who, beaten 4-1, were particularly undone by Peter Lorimer's speed off the mark. Round four took them to Anfield once more where Liverpool were in thunderous form. "At full throttle from start to finish, they lacked only the precision among their forwards for the crucial thrust. Hunter and Madeley were in such form in Leeds' defence that mere passion would not do," wrote Brian James in *The Sunday Times*, who sensed in Bill Shankly's men at the end of a goalless draw an element of resignation; that the replay at Elland Road would be fruitless toil.

If so, they were right. The game's outstanding player was Clarke, who chose to show his talents in all areas, passing, tackling and covering, besides scoring the two sharp goals that thwarted Bill Shankly's team once more.

Even in defeat, Leeds were starting to look imperious. In freezing conditions on a bumpy, rutted pitch at Tottenham, they played football of the highest order, inspiring Tottenham to raise their own game to unaccustomed standards yet succumbing to a goal caused by a solitary lapse when Sprake made a hash of Lorimer's ill-judged backpass which allowed Spurs' centre-forward Martin Chivers to pounce.

The previous week, after beating Sheffield United 1-0, Revie's men had hauled themselves to the top of the first division for the first time, deposing Manchester United. Their occupation of pole position was short-lived; Manchester City, whom Leeds had beaten twice, had come to the fore and capitalised on Leeds' 1-0 defeat at Tottenham. They were to stay top until the end of March as a cluster of teams became enmeshed in an unpredictable race for the title. Meanwhile, Manchester United were on the slide. So convincing in the autumn, they now appeared brittle, the players ill-assorted, the performances incoherent. They had lost five successive league matches before arriving at Elland Road to play Leeds on 19 February.

It was not a place for weaklings. Confronted by the most rapacious team in the league, Manchester were besieged and bothered by performances of pestilential brilliance from almost everyone in a white shirt. They nevertheless clung to life until the 48th minute. Then Clarke swept down the left flank and crossed for Eddie Gray, whose shot was turned on to the post by Stepney. When Mick Jones scored on the rebound, it was the signal for every Leeds outfield player to join in the hunt for Mancunian blood. Made giddy by the runs of Eddie Gray and pummelled by Jones and Lorimer as Bremner, Giles and Clarke gnawed away at the heart of their defence, Manchester United collapsed. Of the closing minutes, with Leeds 5-1 up, Brian Glanville of *The Sunday Times* wrote: "The spectacle was almost that of a matador toying with a weary bull, the delighted roars of the crowd at each new piece of virtuosity the equivalent of the 'olés' of the bullring."

The new virtuosos had annihilated the old. There was more, much more, in this vein to come from Revie's men. Michael Boon of the *Sunday Express* considered their 2-0 win at Cardiff in the FA Cup fifth round the following Saturday as "smooth as cream . . . Leeds are as rich in talent as any club side in the world".

There were few grounds for Southampton to relish visiting Elland Road when Leeds resumed their interest in the league on 4 March. Saddled with one of the most porous defences in the division, the likelihood for The Saints was always that it would be better to travel hopefully than to arrive. Yet it was not the seven goals that Leeds scored but their sustained game of keep-ball, more sadistic than playful, that made the neutrals gasp. Near the end, Leeds passed the ball insolently from one player to another in a swaggering show witnessed by millions watching on television. If forced to sit in the stocks and have rotten tomatoes hurled at them, Southampton could scarcely have been more ridiculed. Leeds' merciless display contained a chilling message: "Dare to stop us!" it seemed to say, to which the Elland Road partisans did indeed chant: "Olé!"

Not only did they bully the weak, Leeds' opponents in the sixth round of the FA Cup two weeks later were Tottenham Hotspur who, although shaky away from White Hart Lane, were

Not just a good side but the greatest: Leeds United fans in triumphalist mood during the sixth-round FA Cup tie against Tottenham at Elland Road in March 1972.

David Harvey, so long in the shadow of Gary Sprake, eventually made the goalkeeper's position his by right.

in better shape than Manchester United and Southampton, and not given to lying down when the stakes were high. Moreover, they were the only team to have beaten Revie's men since November. That Spurs were not swept away by Leeds on the afternoon of 18 March 1972 said much for their courage. Few watching had ever seen football hoisted to such a level of artistry as produced by Leeds in the first 20 minutes. Writers ransacked their stocks of similes and superlatives to try to convey the splendour. Hugh McIlvaney of *The Observer* marvelled as white shirts flooded in on Pat Jennings "with the insistence of surf... their football was breath-taking in its scope and fluency, alive with dazzling improvisations." Brian James of *The Sunday Times* considered that the match had "as many moments of near perfection as football can get." "On this form," wrote Eric Todd of *The Guardian*, "Leeds are irresistible – and when individuals put the team before self-aggrandisement and pool their assets, the result is awesome." Robert Oxby of *The Daily Telegraph* felt that "the awe-inspiring quicksilver grace of Leeds had a majesty and scope unequalled in Britain since Real Madrid defeated Eintracht in 1960."

Paradoxically, the match was a close-run thing. After their opening salvo, Leeds found themselves a goal down but only a prodigious performance in goal from Pat Jennings denied more than two in return. Tottenham gave them a harrowing last few minutes in their frantic quest for an equaliser. Leeds would not, could not, always play this way; critics and misanthropists would have cause once again to deplore their meanness yet performances such as Leeds had produced in March 1972 could only have come from an ardent desire to take the game to new heights; something in the soul.

During those weeks of lyrical football, somehow it seemed to matter a little less who won the FA Cup or the League: Leeds, and Leeds alone, could revel in being acclaimed as the greatest club side in the world. Such was Pat Jennings' opinion having studied them at uncomfortably close quarters. In beating Arsenal 3-0 at Elland Road the following week, Revie's men were fine rather than magical and sometimes uncertain in defence. They were intermittently lethargic against a Nottingham Forest who appeared doomed to relegation but their cause was helped by an injury to Forest goalkeeper Jim Barron and the final margin of victory, 6-1, suggested a rout that did not fairly reflect the match.

The away game on Good Friday at West Ham jolted Leeds out of dreamland. Mid-table, without a desperate need to scrap for points, the Hammers came at Leeds without any inhibitions. Lacking Jones and Giles, Leeds' cutting edge was blunted, the midfield impoverished. By half-time, they were two down. Now they had to remember how to extricate themselves when the going got tough. Cooper marauded down the left, Madeley brought order to midfield and Gray applied the finishing touches, confounding everyone by bending in a shot from the by-line, then seizing on a feeble punch by West Ham goalkeeper Peter Grotier to drive home the equaliser.

Fallible; beatable after all. Derby County, Leeds' opponents on Easter Saturday who had been spared a Good Friday fixture, would have taken note. Giles, drafted back into the side though still unfit, was ill-equipped to check and counter the thrusts of John O'Hare, Kevin Hector and Archie Gemmill. After 16 minutes, a blunder from Bremner saw Leeds concede possession; Alan Durban crossed to O'Hare and his smart header beat Gary Sprake. Thereafter, Leeds always had to chase the game. Another second-half raid by O'Hare saw him shoot against Sprake and the hapless Norman Hunter ran the ball into his own goal. Suddenly awkward questions were being asked. What were Leeds in midfield without Giles? Who could compensate for the absence of Mick Jones? What of their much-vaunted strength in depth? Malcolm Allison, the Manchester City manager, was unimpressed and declared himself bored with talk about Leeds: "They'll win nothing . . . they hit a freak run at home against teams which forgot to take their defences on the field."

Back at full strength once more, Leeds beat Huddersfield Town 3-1 in their next match at Elland Road, though they were made to sweat for victory. At Stoke the following week, the home side was under-strength and still basking in their League Cup Final victory while having a breather before their scrap with Arsenal in the FA Cup semi-final. Leeds won 3-0 with patience, power and, ultimately, with ease but having paid an awful price. Seven minutes from time, with the game settled, Terry Cooper collided with Stoke defender John Marsh and broke his left shin. The England left-back, who had so often given Leeds injections of vitality through his surging, bold performances, was destined never to recover a regular place in the team. What might have been a swift rehabilitation was prevented because Cooper's production of bone calcium was unusually slow.

Despite punishing efforts to regain fitness, Cooper was to miss all the 1972/73 campaign and played only fitfully in the two following seasons before transferring to Middlesbrough in March, 1975. Cooper suffered greatly to get back in shape. It was a year before he could resume training with the team, one in which he became increasingly isolated from his colleagues and drawn towards his family. Working in the sports shop he had bought with his accountant kept him busy on Saturdays; he saw only four of 70 matches the team played without him during that time. "The lads haven't altered but I've lost touch. Though this has taught me patience – never to take anything for granted again," he said.

Above all, Cooper was determined to regain his England place and play in the 1974 World Cup. It was not to be. Although his career was to continue with Middlesbrough, Bristol City, Bristol Rovers and Doncaster Rovers, Terry Cooper's days as the world's finest left-back were over.

Leeds' opponents in the FA Cup semi-final were Birmingham City, second division standard-bearers, who had travelled to Hillsborough in good form and good spirits. Defeat, while it stopped short of being humiliation, was utterly comprehensive and inevitable after Jones and Lorimer put Leeds 2-0 up after 27 minutes. Thereafter, Birmingham's mental and physical energies were largely confined to containing Revie's men who, prompted by Giles and Hunter striking deep passes to all corners, played with the arrogance of a team used to getting its own way. Victory was sealed by a third goal, scored by Mick Jones, on 65 minutes. Now Leeds' dream of the double was down to four league games and a Cup Final. "If we do it, I feel we should not be classed as on a par with Real Madrid but just as Leeds United," Revie said.

Still the championship contenders jostled, seemingly in command one week, inexplicably fallible the next. Newcastle, becalmed in mid-table, seemed determined to interfere in the race: they gave Derby County a bloody nose by beating them on Easter Monday and then did the same to Revie's men on 19 April with a lively, industrious performance that was settled by a spectacular headed goal from Malcolm MacDonald nine minutes from time. Three days later at West Bromwich, after a stern contest in which a light ball, bumpy pitch and gusty wind made orderly football difficult, Leeds squeezed the result essential to their ambitions through a penalty scored by Giles after Mick Jones was felled in the area by two Albion defenders. It put Leeds in buoyant mood for their final home game, against Chelsea, on 1 May. Although without Eddie Gray, all other working parts appeared in good order; the irresistible swinging rhythm was still there. Chelsea were combative, vigorous opponents but two crisp goals, from Bremner on 20 minutes and Jones in the 75th, saw Leeds through.

The fog had cleared at last. Victory over Arsenal in the Centenary Cup Final on 6 May would give Leeds the first part of the double; a draw at Wolverhampton two days later the second. Revie, who had spent many of his early years bemoaning the apathy and fickleness of the Leeds public, now sensed for the first time that Elland Road had the aura of belonging to a great club: "You could feel the buzz beforehand, the electricity right through the crowd."

The prospect of another Wembley final against the Gunners was, among some pessimists, a source of foreboding. The thuggish League Cup Final of 1968 had not been forgotten and, for all that they had won the double the previous season, Arsenal's football was frequently primitive. Leeds, whose game had evolved many stages further, remained susceptible to provocation. Ostensibly, Leeds were at full strength. David Harvey was preferred to Gary Sprake in goal; Johnny Giles, Eddie Gray and Allan Clarke came through fitness tests on the

Determination and control;
Billy Bremner in charge as
always.

morning of the game, though it soon became clear that Giles, carrying a groin strain, was severely below par. Leeds were to assert their authority in other areas, thankful that Alan Ball, so often the fulcrum of Arsenal's attack, was less effervescent than usual.

The pessimists must have thought their worst fears justified when, in the first minute, Arsenal left-back Bob McNab scythed down Peter Lorimer and was booked for his pains. Gray was fouled twice in a minute and before the game was over Hunter, Bremner and Arsenal's Charlie George also had their names taken. Such sporadic unpleasantness led to the final being unduly maligned. There was much good, rippling football, most of it from Leeds. Lorimer, as he had done for much of the season, combined power with delicacy; Clarke was as dangerous as a cobra; Reaney, Charlton and Hunter policing the Arsenal spear-head of George, Radford and Kennedy, were marvellously solid; Jones, as ever, the tireless workhorse.

Arsenal, although outplayed, had their electrifying moments, none more so than when, after a sophisticated bout of passing, Charlie George struck a volley that clattered the Leeds crossbar. By then, Leeds had scored their single precious goal. It came in the 54th minute and was of theatrical splendour: a sweeping move down the right that involved Madeley, Lorimer and the tireless Jones. Riding a challenge from McNab near the corner flag, Jones whipped the ball across the penalty area and Clarke, sprinting in to meet it, dispatched a high velocity header past Geoff Barnett. It was a goal fit to win the FA Cup. The air was rent with

the roar of Yorkshire jubilation. Leeds, as if minded to seek a place in history as the greatest of all Wembley showmen, resumed play with a swagger, though with only a goal lead to protect, courted potential disaster with the bravado of some of their passing.

Disaster befell Mick Jones almost on full-time, with the Cup won. Leading a final assault on the Arsenal goal, Jones stumbled over goalkeeper Geoff Barnett and fell heavily on his left arm. As the match ended amid cacophonous celebrations on the terraces, Jones lay in agony, his elbow dislocated. It took Norman Hunter to help the Leeds centre-forward, his arm strapped, up the steps to receive a winner's medal from the Queen. Wembley had seen few more poignant sights.

Leeds' challenge for the league title at Wolverhampton 48 hours later was to be prosecuted without their fearless target man and with several walking wounded. Gray and Clarke each took to the field with a thigh heavily strapped; Bates took Jones' place, neat and willing as ever but without the same ability to disrupt and unhinge determined defences. Molineux, with 53,000 squeezed in and thousands more locked out, was a bubbling cauldron as Wolves elected to play with as much fire and passion as if their own title aspirations were at stake. Two penalties denied them when Shaw appeared to handle the ball in the area, once in each half; three astounding saves by Parkes: well might Leeds consider that fate had turned against them once more as, driven on ferociously by Bremner, they drew on their deepest reserves of energy. Unfortunately for them, not only were Wolves brave, they were fatally

Opposite. Flags, scarves and banners: the pageantry of a great occasion. Leeds, led by Don Revie, and Arsenal, led by Bertie Mee, take the field for the 1972 Centenary Cup Final.
Below. The view from in front. Norman Hunter jumps for joy as Clarke scores.

Below. Full time sees Mick Jones lying in agony on the Wembley turf after dislocating a shoulder following his collision with Geoff Barnett.

Opposite. And about time too: Leeds skipper Billy Bremner holds the FA Cup aloft.

incisive. After a goalmouth mêlée that ensued from a Wolves corner six minutes before half-time, Francis Munro scored with a stabbing shot and, with 25 minutes left, Wolves pounced again, Derek Dougan scoring on the end of a swift breakaway.

Regardless, Leeds blazed on. Almost from the restart, Giles swung out an inspired pass to the left, Madeley crossed and Bremner snapped up a goal from close in. Thereafter the Wolves defence was called upon to perform miracles of salvage but there was no way through, not even for Bremner, playing like a demon, chasing every cause. It was, reflected Geoffrey Green in *The Times*, "a brilliant failure to add to their distinguished record. Leeds died like heroes". How far had Leeds been affected both by the euphoria and the strains of Saturday? Eric Todd wondered in *The Guardian*. "This will go down as one of the bravest footballing failures of all time: indeed, I would hesitate to call it a failure at all," he said.

Derby County, on tour in Majorca, had won the League Championship without a further kick. Brian Clough's team were popular winners, they had played some excellent football but the belief in Leeds was that the second-best team had won. Revie was distraught at having seen his place in history snatched away. "It's just too much. We should have had at least three penalties. When decisions like that go against you, what can you do?" he said. The celebrations of Saturday had turned into a wake. Where next? supporters wondered. How many more tumultuous seasons? How much more could the old troops give?

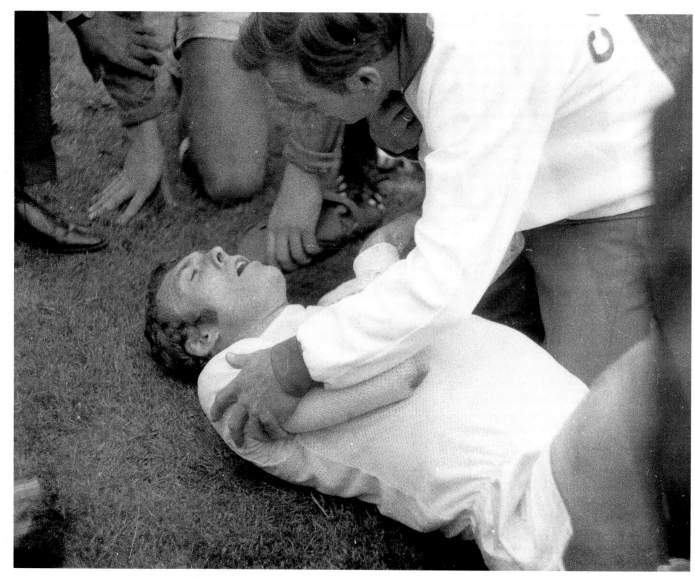

Revie's grand team embarked on the 1972/73 season looking somewhat shaky on its feet. Hunter and Clarke, as punishment for a rash of bookings collected in the previous campaign, were suspended. There was no Terry Cooper. Jack Charlton, now 37, could not last indefinitely. Mick Jones' proneness to injury would constantly sap Leeds of forward strength. To stiffen the defence, Revie bought, as a small job-lot from Huddersfield, Trevor Cherry to replace Cooper and centre-half Roy Ellam as cover for Jack Charlton. In attack, the abrasive but skilful Joe Jordan, signed by Revie from Morton for £15,000 in 1970 on Bobby Collins' recommendation, emerged from reserve-team football to master the rough old trade of being a centre-forward.

With so many enforced changes of personnel, Leeds could hardly expect to be at their silken best. Cherry, though less naturally gifted than Cooper, settled in at left-back, essentially a hard-tackling ball winner with attacking instincts. Terry Yorath, also emerging from the reserves, had many of the same characteristics but it was his ill-fortune in future seasons to shoulder the burden of replacing Johnny Giles. Substituting a committed journeyman for a maestro was never a fair exchange and, however hard he tried, the young Welshman found it impossible to win over a section of disgruntled Leeds supporters.

While Joe Jordan took to football at the top level as if born to it, poor Roy Ellam floundered quite out of his depth and returned to Huddersfield following a season in which the centre-half problem was never resolved. Ellam, Paul Madeley, Jack Charlton and the young Scottish reserve Gordon McQueen all took turns at number five. The career of John Faulkner, bought from Sutton United after hounding Mick Jones in the FA Cup two seasons earlier, never got going after he broke a kneecap in only his second game against Manchester City and he had been sold to Luton by March 1972.

Gary Sprake, finally out of favour, was to depart at the start of the 1973/74 season, transferred to Birmingham City for £70,000. Belatedly, Revie decided that for all Sprake's talents, David Harvey had a safer pair of hands. Harvey, as dedicated and brave a goalkeeper as any in the country, had endured seven seasons of reserve-team football as Sprake's understudy. It was something of a miracle that Don Revie managed to cling on to him: within a year of sampling regular first division football, Harvey was capped by Scotland.

The core of the team remained. It had taken more than pep talks after so many shattering defeats to keep everyone together: Revie had also had a deft touch when negotiating personal terms, as Billy Bremner recalls. "At the end of the season, you'd get options on your contract. I would go in and ask for a rise. Then just as I'd walk in, he'd say: 'Wee man I'm going to increase your money' and tell you the amount. He'd give you more than you were going to ask for but a bit later, you'd suddenly think: 'He's done you, he's got you under contract again,' but you think he's a good guy because he's upped your wages."

On opening day, Revie's men endured a 4-0 drubbing at Chelsea but not all was as it seemed from the scoreline: after 25 minutes, Harvey was carried off the field suffering from concussion, forcing Leeds to field Peter Lorimer in goal. Almost at the same time, Mick Jones had hobbled off with an ankle injury. It was no day for Leeds to be fairly judged.

As if to prove the point, they won five and drew three of the next eight league matches, though with injuries disrupting team selection and even the ever-present Bremner less than match-fit, they rarely displayed the utter conviction that had been last season's hallmark.

Jordan's apprenticeship at centre-forward was giving grounds for optimism and he crowned a robust and skilful display in the 3-3 home draw against Ipswich on 23 August with two goals. Off-key, perhaps, yet Leeds' profitable run put them up among the leaders. After

Opposite. A word too many: Billy Bremner was sometimes over-keen to argue Leeds' case with referees.
Above. The names evoke great memories. Leeds United's encounters with Bill Shankly's Liverpool team were always momentous. Liverpool won this 2-1.

Above. Speed, determination and tough tackling were the qualities that saw left-back Trevor Cherry break into the England team in 1976. Though less gifted than his predecessor, Terry Cooper, Cherry was a loyal and durable servant.

Opposite. Here we go again. The programme cover from Leeds United's FA Cup semifinal against Wolves in April 1973. Leeds won 1-0.

nine matches, they had 13 points and trailed Everton and Ipswich Town only on goal average.

However, the feeling persisted that cracks existed which hitherto had been papered over. Confirmation came in a hectic game at Newcastle that yielded four goals in the first eight minutes, four bookings, and saw the Magpies victorious with a winner from Malcolm MacDonald on the hour. Petulant rather than decisive, Leeds had struggled throughout the afternoon to quell Newcastle's constant surging attacks.

When Revie's men lost 1-2 at home to Liverpool the following week, the obituarists got to work. "Leeds beginning to wither with age," intoned *The Guardian*. Eric Todd wrote: "I think they must accept that Giles and Charlton are past their peak, and that Bremner's overworked batteries are running low . . . Leeds have achieved many great things but now, as in the instance of Belshazzar of old, the writing is on the wall." Despite a magnificent goal on the half hour from Jones' acrobatic scissors kick, Liverpool pounced on two lax pieces of Leeds play to win the game.

Two successive league defeats: "The beginning of the end," proclaimed the prophets of doom but the following week Leeds were at home to the champions, Derby County, and beat them 5-0. "With Giles and Bremner at their most masterful and Gray, that most delicate of wingers, back in the side, it was like old times at Elland Road," wrote Tony Pawson of *The Observer*. "Bremner is far from an extinct volcano, the eruptions of energy less spectacular perhaps but the subtlety even clearer to see." Possibly reports of Leeds United's lingering death had been exaggerated.

Prodigious occasionally, mopping up in most other games efficiently: it had the old familiar ring as Leeds made steady, if not always bewitching progress in the league but also in the League Cup (beating Burnley 4-0 then Aston Villa 3-1 on aggregate) and in the European Cup Winners Cup, defeating the Turkish team Ankargucu (2-1 on aggregate) and the East Germans Carl Zeiss Jena (2-0). However, they lacked the consistency that had made them irresistible. After the rout of Derby, Leeds fans were alarmed to see their team pegged back and put firmly on the defensive for spells of the 1-1 home draw against Coventry two weeks later. Yet a week later at Wolverhampton, all the old authority was there in their 2-0 victory, achieved by goals from Gray and Lorimer in the first half hour. "Leeds took vacant possession of Molineux, shutting Wolverhampton out of the game as completely as if they had locked them in the dressing-room and pocketed the key . . . at last they are beginning to show their wonderfully co-ordinated flair and technique," wrote David Lacey in *The Guardian*.

By the end of November, with the league season approaching its halfway point, none of the leading pack had the aura of champions. The leaders, Liverpool, were impregnable at Anfield, having won all nine home games. They had also ended Leeds' exploits in the League Cup winning a replayed fourth-round tie at Elland Road with a headed goal from Kevin Keegan in the last minute. Leeds, often giving the impression that they were distracted by weightier matters, had fared abysmally in the competition in almost every season apart from 1968, the year in which they won it.

After 19 matches, Liverpool had 28 points. Leeds, in second place, had 26 but a 2-1 defeat on 2 December at Arsenal, who had been third, saw the two sides swap places. Despite all future fluctuations of form, twists and turns, the pattern at the top had been set: here were the three horses in the race, the nature of which was to be pursuit of Liverpool.

Leeds' campaign to retain the FA Cup began laboriously with two 1-1 draws against Norwich, their opponents in the third round. The smouldering superiority of Revie's men ignited in the second replay at Villa Park. Allan Clarke, scorer of a fine hat-trick in the first 20 minutes, was the chief tormenter as Leeds ran riot, teasing, tormenting, parading their acute skills unopposed. Beaten 5-0, Norwich had been let off lightly yet five days later, in their fourth-round tie against third division Plymouth Argyle, Leeds, with Billy Bremner suspended, seemed shorn of their powers. They had to to toil for their 2-1 victory in which all goals came during a six-minute spell midway through the second half.

Continued progress in the FA Cup revived the spectre of a battle on three fronts. Invariably, such burdensome quests had ended in tears for Revie's men. A nagging feeling that they were never fully abreast of the race for the League Championship was reinforced by a resounding 2-0 defeat at Leicester City on 10 February, the day Arsenal became the first team to win at Anfield. Leeds had felt the loss of Bremner and soon suspension would deprive them of Norman Hunter, their other great linchpin, whose ferocious efforts that season had already earned seven bookings.

In the FA Cup fifth-round tie against West Bromwich at Elland Road, Leeds once more appeared to have recovered their edge. The return of Eddie Gray on the left wing helped restore balance and width: invariably, Leeds were the richer for his flair and, as if to celebrate being back, Gray tortured Albion's defenders with irrepressible ball control and crosses that unhinged their best-laid plans. Elsewhere, Leeds were sharp and alert, making the most of Albion's mistakes, and winning 2-0 with goals from Allan Clarke.

Towards the end of March, Leeds began to show signs of being oppressed by all their obligations, a month in which they were seen in all shades and hues: brilliant, indifferent; thuggish, then on their best behaviour. The complexion of their 3-2 win against Derby County at the Baseball Ground on 3 March suggested that the 5-0 victory at Elland Road in October had not assuaged Leeds' sense of having been robbed of the championship. It was a vengeful, violent encounter of more than 50 fouls and, no doubt, a startling league début for young Gordon McQueen but Leeds snatched the game via two penalties and Clarke's predatory goal that followed a poor back-pass from Colin Todd.

The fall-out, numerous lurid headlines and hard words, bode ill for a rematch on 17 March in the FA Cup sixth round. For their misdemeanours, various Leeds players had become threatened with suspension: Hunter and Cherry had each been booked eight times; Bremner, Clarke, Lorimer and Jones had also collected a fistful of cautions yet all the old warhorses were eligible for a second expedition to the Baseball Ground. This time, however, the fight was clean, even though Cherry (who, with Clarke, was about to start a two-match ban) earned his ninth booking. In cool, calculating mood, Leeds attacked in strength, scored after half an hour, then retreated to hold the fort though still burst into enemy territory with frequent rapier-like thrusts.

It could almost have been one of Leeds' European matches: a tight, tactical tussle in a far-off country. As it was, ten days earlier they had used their opponents in the Cup Winners Cup quarter-final, Rapid Bucharest, for target practice. Eric Todd of *The Guardian* regarded Leeds' 5-0 demolition of the Rumanians as among their greatest performances in European competition. It was certainly a triumph for total football and patience in the face of savage tackling. The return leg appeared a formality, though Bates' opening goal after 62 seconds suggested that the pathologically cautious Don Revie thought otherwise. On the night Leeds won 3-1; on aggregate 8-1.

By the end of the month, the League Championship appeared to be drifting out of reach. Three days after letting slip a goal lead in their 1-1 draw at West Bromwich, on 31 March, Leeds produced possibly their most pallid performance of the season in losing 1-0 to Manchester City at Maine Road.

Although Revie's men still had two games in hand, Liverpool's seven-point lead now appeared insuperable. Moreover, five of Leeds' last eight games were away: they seemed no more likely to make a prodigious late run than did Liverpool suddenly to fall apart.

On 7 April, however, Leeds were full of their old vim for the FA Cup semi-final against Wolves, even without Hunter, Gray and, for much of the match, Charlton. High tension and a boisterous wind did much to disrupt coherent football in the first half, though each side had their chances. In the second half, the tempo picked up and the football unfurled with first Wolves, then Leeds, having spasms of intense pressure. Midway through the second half, the Leeds attacks, led by Lorimer, became a bombardment. It was he, who at the height of the blitz, hooked the ball into the goalmouth and precipitated the mêlée from which Billy Bremner barged in the only goal of the game.

Official Programme   FA Cup Semi Final

LEEDS UNITED
v
WOLVERHAMPTON WANDERERS

7th April 1973 at Maine Road, Manchester 10p

Four days later, Leeds looked irritable and jittery as they faced Hajduk Split in the first leg of their European Cup Winners Cup semi-final. They allowed themselves to be provoked, as they had not against Rapid Bucharest and gave the ball away with dismaying frequency, as if their composure had been eroded either by the fixture pile-up or else through contemplating the enormity of everything at stake. Allan Clarke was the key figure in a scuffling ill-favoured match, embarking on a splendid run past several Hajduk defenders to score the only goal of the game in the first half and then being sent off in the second for retaliation. That, rather than his delicious goal, epitomised the evening.

Two weeks later, Revie's men were in dour and introverted mood during the second leg in Yugoslavia. Any dreams they harboured of winning the league had evaporated following a 1-0 defeat at Elland Road by Manchester United, and losing 2-0 at Anfield to Liverpool, the champions-elect. The narrowness of Leeds' first-leg lead and loss of form reduced their game to a tedious exercise in stonewalling. Clarke had been automatically suspended following his sending off but Hajduk lacked the wit to prise them open. For Don Revie, the job was well done: the joyless display had given them the chance of becoming the first British club to win the FA Cup and a European trophy in the same season.

Their opponents at Wembley were second division Sunderland, whose fortunes had undergone a revolution since appointing Bob Stokoe as manager a few months earlier. Unquenchable spirit and the passion engendered by massive support had helped propel them to the final, though there had been doubters to the last: few had given a penny for their chances when they drew Arsenal in the semi-final. Stokoe was a populist manager, at one with his people: they, as much as anything, were his motivation for wanting to win the Cup. He was also driven by an intense personal dislike of Don Revie going back eleven years to Stokoe's days as manager of Bury and a game against Leeds at Gigg Lane in April 1962. Revie, Stokoe later claimed, had tried to bribe him to "throw" the match, so desperate was the Leeds manager for points to save his team from relegation to the third division.

Stokoe conducted a little psychological warfare against Revie beforehand, drawing the media's attention to the Leeds players' constant harassment of referees. "Ken Burns [the Cup Final referee] won't allow that," Stokoe declared. He also grumbled publicly about Leeds being given the better dressing-rooms and the choice of the better end for their supporters. Nonsense it may have been but it was designed to make it harder for Revie's men to capture the hearts of the uncommitted.

As Stokoe knew, Revie was prone to paranoia. On 5 May, the day of the final, there was a pointed contrast between the light-headed exuberance of the Sunderland camp and the stiff buttoned-up demeanour of Revie and his players. Leeds had won at Wembley the previous season yet seemed infected by their manager's insecurity. Unlike the previous year when their support overwhelmed that of Arsenal, there was a strong sense that everyone in the land save for the Leeds faithful was rooting for Sunderland. Peter Lorimer recalled Revie's highly-strung state: "Eddie Gray and I were going downstairs in our hotel and a photographer took a picture. Don grabbed the camera off him and nearly threw it through the window. He didn't like pictures of his team being taken before games. It was one of his superstitions."

The atmosphere inside Wembley bore witness to the underdogs being the people's favourites. During a match played in intermittent rain and sunshine, Leeds had the lions' share of possession, abundant chances and the finer players confronting a goalkeeper who was palpably jittery – yet contrived to lose. The biggest FA Cup Final upset of all time defied all analysis. If Sunderland goalkeeper Jim Montgomery, in the words of Brian Glanville, treated the ball as if he feared it contained high explosive, he also made the finest save of the game: a save more celebrated than the solitary goal that won Sunderland the cup. It came midway

through the second half, at the end of a frenzied bout of Leeds pressure; a superhuman piece of goalkeeping that drained much of the spirit from Revie's men.

Sunderland led after scoring in the 32nd minute. Until then, they had been pinned back by waves of Leeds attacks, their goal frequently at risk. When they broke out and Vic Halom shot optimistically from 30 yards, Harvey cautiously tipped the ball over the bar. How was he to know what calamity would ensue from the corner? When it came over, Vic Halom was first to it, flicking on the ball to Ian Porterfield. From this simplest of moves, the Leeds defence was horribly wrong-footed. Porterfield brought the ball under control and smashed it into the Leeds net. The celebrations were tumultuous and, pepped-up by self-belief, Sunderland picked up their game, though twice Leeds should have equalised, through Clarke and Lorimer.

In the second half, playing controlled and occasionally furious football, Revie's men subjected Sunderland to pressure so intense that many a more talented side might have wilted. The crescendo came on 65 minutes. From an intricate passing movement involving Giles and Jones, Reaney knocked in an inviting centre that Trevor Cherry headed goalwards with aplomb. Montgomery beat it away, only for the ball to fall to Peter Lorimer. He struck it with his mighty right foot then turned away to rejoice at his easy pickings. For a split second all the world, like Lorimer himself, thought the equaliser had arrived but somehow, Montgomery himself hardly knew how, the Sunderland goalkeeper flipped himself up off the ground and deflected Lorimer's strike on to the underside of the bar. Immediately there was a sense of the Leeds hurricane having blown itself out.

In the last twenty minutes, chances fell to both sides but for all the elegant promptings of Madeley, the scurrying of Bremner and Giles, there was no way through for Leeds. Dave Watson, above all, gave a gigantic display at the heart of the Sunderland defence. It was a day for romantics.

Revie's men had eleven days to regroup and repair their shattered morale before the European Cup Winners Cup Final against AC Milan in Greece. The culmination of their season was taking on a horribly familiar pattern: sweat, toil and tears but no glory. The omens were not good for their final big game: injuries and suspension had deprived them of Bremner, Clarke, Giles and Eddie Gray. Alas, not only did the weakened Leeds team have AC Milan as opponents, they were also, it appeared, up against the Greek referee.

As much as anything, the seeming partiality of Christos Michas dictated the passage of the rain-soaked 1973 European Cup Winners Cup Final. In the fourth minute, he penalised Madeley for an innocuous-looking tackle near the left-hand edge of the Leeds penalty area. The resulting indirect free kick from Chiarugi took a deflection and shot into the Leeds net off the foot of a post. Almost nothing of the Milan attack was seen for the remaining 86 minutes as they conducted one of the most notorious rearguard actions in European club competition. From time to time, this was carried out with ruthless desperation. But referee Michas was their guardian angel. Three times he rejected claims for penalties that looked irrefutable: in the first half when Mick Jones was floored in the area; in the second when a Reaney centre was clearly handled and Jones, once more, was sandwiched and buffeted to the ground. Leeds, led by Lorimer, Jones and Jordan probed and pressed incessantly but could not pick a way through. They could have given no more and by the end could stomach no more. Two minutes from time, Hunter was sent off for retaliation, overcome by frustration at Leeds' failure and at having been being hacked about by Italian defenders all evening.

The Greek crowd sympathised with Leeds, cheering them off the field as if they were the victors. To almost everyone except their supporters, AC Milan's victory was considered debased currency. As for Mr Michas it emerged that UEFA had seen fit to put him in charge, even though the previous year he had been banned for three months following an aberrant display during a league game between two Greek teams. Never again would he referee a game of importance but that was scant comfort to Leeds United. The result stood: Revie's men had reached out for three trophies and ended up with nothing but a handful of dust.

Robbery with violence. Once more, Norman Hunter is fouled by an AC Milan defender in the 1973 European Cup Winners Cup Final. Leeds lost 1-0 and Hunter was sent off for retaliation just before time.

> *"Leeds' emotions live close to the surface, their character constantly under stress from their own creativity, their persistent injury problems symptomatic not of damaged muscles but overstressed minds."*
>
> *John Samuel, The Guardian*

Once more the critics scented decay at Elland Road. Leeds United's defining characteristics had been continuity and the single-mindedness with which they went about everything. All this had come from Don Revie but there had been occasional tremors when stories emerged of approaches to him from other clubs. No-one knew quite how many offers Revie had spurned but, over the years, they were spread from as far apart as Sunderland and Torino.

Leeds' cause in the European Cup Winners Cup Final had hardly been helped by the fact that on the eve of the match, the press had been buzzing with news of their manager's impending departure to Everton. This time, it looked for real: beforehand, Revie had flown to the south of France for talks with the Everton chairman John Moores. If he did go, as looked likely, would not the break-up of his redoubtable team inevitably follow? Eric Todd of *The Guardian* felt that Revie realised he could do no more for his players, nor the players for him. "He surely realises that his ship needs a refit and, after it, a new ship's company," wrote Todd. "This may be the breaker's yard for Leeds United's most successful combination."

Revie stalled and, as the days went on, it was clear that something was amiss. For whatever reason, financial or a passionate belief that his team was not yet played out, he elected to stay.

There remained much to do, beginning with atonement for the disciplinary transgressions of the fierce 1972/73 campaign. The FA had imposed a £3,000 fine, to be suspended only if the club cleaned up its act. Revie began a charm offensive, promising better behaviour and asking for everyone's help in achieving the objective. The club also appointed its first full-time public relations officer, Peter Fay. Using the platform of a regular column in the new-look club programme, Revie shared his thoughts with the world.

The behaviour of his players in 1972/73 had been castigated not only by the FA but by the media and Derby manager Brian Clough, not least after the recent rasping league game at the Baseball Ground. Clough caused offence at a dinner held in Peter Lorimer's honour by proclaiming that the Leeds winger habitually fell over when he had not been kicked, and spent much time protesting when there was nothing to grumble about. Revie affected not to know what everyone was on about. "I plead not guilty to being a member of the destruction squad. But I am slowly sinking in a surfeit of bad publicity. I appeal to the press to start writing about the good things again," came the disingenuous request.

The good tidings from Leeds were that from the reserves, shoots of new growth had forced their way up into the first team. Jack Charlton, at almost 38 and after 772 games over 22 years, had retired after a career that blossomed magnificently in its autumn, departing to manage Middlesbrough. The burden of filling the vacuum was thrust upon the precocious Gordon McQueen, bought from St Mirren for just £30,000 in September 1972. Guided by old hands such as Reaney and Hunter, the statuesque McQueen matured at an astonishing speed. Terry Yorath was now assimilated into the first team set-up and also emerging was Frank Gray, younger brother of Eddie, a left-sided midfielder rich in natural ability. Meanwhile, the storming form of Joe Jordan compensated for the recurring absence of Mick Jones.

As if their mission in life was to confound all who felt they were past it, Revie's men set about the opposition in August and September with a brio that recalled the heady days of March 1972. On opening day, Everton – now managed by Billy Bingham – were the visitors. Leeds tucked in with relish. Bremner and Giles, of whom it had been frequently muttered that their powers were waning, each responded by striking magnificent goals in a 3-1 win that might have been more emphatic save for the old faults of arrogance and over-elaboration. At

Opposite. Is it a goalkeeper or a work of modern art? David Harvey takes a stylish tumble as he gathers the ball. Above. Height, presence and a fine touch for one so tall: many were astonished by the speed at which Gordon McQueen, once a winger, learned his trade at centre-half.

Arsenal three days later, they showed buoyant spirit and skill to overcome the blow of losing a goal within 70 seconds, retrieving then winning the game with second-half goals from Lorimer and Madeley.

Returning to north London the following Saturday, they picked off a flaccid Tottenham side with fluent ease, scoring three goals in the first 28 minutes then revelling in the opportunity to flaunt their talents. Clarke, who had begun the season with a tremendous flourish, was tormenter-in-chief during Leeds' next virtuoso performance, carving Wolves to pieces in their 4-1 victory at Elland Road. Elegant, assured victories over Birmingham (3-0) and at Wolverhampton (2-0) followed.

The ageing and cantankerous side that so recently seemed fit only for the breaker's yard had metamorphosed into a rejuvenated team which looked as if it might only be halted by opponents resorting to grievous bodily harm. As they recalled their seventh victory in succession in a 2-1 win at Southampton, John Arlott, reporting for *The Guardian* was struck not only by Leeds' mastery of the game but also the even-tempered way they went about their business: "Wearing the white strip of a blameless life . . . it was all so controlled, almost amiable . . . so free from the aura of violence they used to generate."

Alas, all changed when Manchester United came to town for the eighth game. Now lacking the illustrious triumvirate of Best, Law and Charlton, it was Manchester who came cast in the role of wicked queen to Leeds United's Snow White. Indeed, if the all-conquering run of Revie's men was to be sabotaged by grievous bodily harm, the men from Manchester arrived ready to wield the strong arm. They became the first side to take a point off Leeds with an "amalgam of rank foul play, time-wasting and negative tactics," commented Rob Hughes in *The Sunday Times*. Amid the frenzied atmosphere and thuggery, Jordan spoiled Leeds' unblemished record of 1973/74 in becoming the first to receive a caution. It was as if

someone had reminded an innocent that the world was a wicked place and it was especially poignant that the vulnerably brilliant Eddie Gray sustained an injury which precluded him from playing in all but one of the season's remaining fixtures.

Leeds were much more wary, cautious and prone to falling back on defence in their 1-0 victory at Norwich the following week but the next side to deprive them of a point, Stoke City, did so the following Saturday with honour, in a splendid, even-tempered 1-1 draw that showed Leeds had recovered most of their form and some of their humour. Reminders that their peers were not all pushovers were issued frequently to Leeds in October. Ipswich Town dispatched them smartly out of the League Cup, beating them 2-0 at Portman Road in a lively match which suggested that even if Leeds didn't care too much, playing competitive flowing football had become instinctive. Their next league game at Leicester City, a 2-2 draw in which Revie's men recovered an early two-goal deficit, also crackled with life and was the richer for the inability of either side to dominate.

If they could beat Liverpool at Elland Road on 20 October, Leeds fans could reassure themselves that their extravagant early surge for the title was genuine. For Leeds, performances – and results – against Liverpool remained the litmus test: they had lost to Bill Shankly's men three times the previous season and dearly wanted to redress the balance. A single goal separated the sides in a match that was hard, fast and clean. Beginning with Allan Clarke, and finished by a Mick Jones header, Leeds succeeded in pulling the Liverpool defence apart with an inspired move involving Bremner and Lorimer in which punishingly accurate passes were swept from one side of the pitch to the other.

Usually, Leeds managed to harness their talents to find a way through. Otherwise, they could rely on a stout rearguard, as in goalless draws against Burnley and Derby. Interspersed with these barren encounters, the style in which Leeds fashioned home wins over West Ham

Opposite. Breathing fire, centre-forward Joe Jordan hurls himself into the fray. In time, he became a first-class replacement for the injury-prone Mick Jones.
Below. *Gray stands for grace. Like older brother Eddie, Frank Gray had profuse talent.*

(4-1) and Coventry (3-0) was ample evidence that if the climate permitted, they would strive for perfection. They dismantled the Hammers with a combination of direct assault and intricacy, every move cunningly plotted and superbly executed. For Alan Dunn of *The Guardian*, the display against Coventry would "linger long in a memory starved of such nourishment in recent years. Coventry were reduced to bemused men by the majesty of Leeds' football . . . the Leeds players found a level of understanding that was, at times, otherworldly."

It was their coherence, their ability to execute the simple and the intricate with equal aplomb that moved critics to such effusion. Even on ice and snow and with a rock-hard surface beneath such as prevailed at Elland Road for the 2-2 draw against Queen's Park Rangers on 1 December, both teams rose above the hostile conditions to provide a spectacular exhibition of soccer arts and crafts. "The romantic side of me hopes that we might go through the entire season without losing a single league match," wrote Revie in his column.

A week later at Ipswich, Leeds equalled Liverpool's modern times record of 19 unbeaten matches from the start of the season in emphatic style. Ipswich, a progressive side growing in assurance from season to season, had nothing in their armoury with which to repel Leeds at full throttle. Revie's men won 3-0 and the maligned Yorath, who scored one fine goal and helped make the second for Mick Jones, had one of his best games.

The following week, Liverpool's record fell at Stamford Bridge. In beating Chelsea 2-1, Leeds showed for the umpteenth time that accuracy and understanding were their paramount virtues. There was a temptation to think the League Championship was becoming a parade, a one-horse race, that Revie's men were invincible and their lead unassailable, particularly after they shed an interest in the UEFA Cup, losing to the Portuguese side Vitoria Setubal 3-2 on aggregate. Injuries were the ostensible reason for Revie fielding a side peppered with reserves in the 3-1 away defeat; probably he didn't care too much.

The League Championship, on the other hand, demanded his best attention at all times. By the end of December, Leeds had played 23 matches and gained 39 points. Liverpool, their nearest challengers, were eight points adrift. The year end saw Leeds' unbeaten record subjected to an onslaught by relegation-threatened Birmingham City. Often outrun, trailing to a 21st-minute goal by Bob Latchford, and scarcely resembling football gods save for David Harvey who produced heroics in goal, deliverance came three minutes from time when a long ball from Paul Madeley found Lorimer who galloped down the right and then crossed to Jordan in space. The centre-forward had time to steady himself before driving firmly past Sprake.

The relief was overwhelming but the unbeaten record was becoming an emotional burden. Tension was creeping into Leeds' games and it became more onerous to keep the momentum with the prolonged absences of Cooper, Giles and Gray. That Leeds still managed to show creativity on their left flank spoke much for an ability to improvise and the qualities of Madeley, Yorath and, earlier, Mick Bates. Hunter, as ever, was playing with the heart of a lion.

Three days later in the 1-1 home draw against Tottenham, signs were that the well-oiled machine was starting to creak. Where there had been certainty, now Leeds dithered; diffidence had replaced confidence. In the FA Cup third round, Revie's men were twice run close by Wolves, though in the course of two excellent matches looked to have recovered their form. The issue was settled in a replay at Elland Road with a goal from Mick Jones after the two sides had drawn 1-1 at Molineux. Without Giles, McQueen, Cooper, Clarke, Bates and Gray, Leeds still managed to overcome Southampton at Elland Road on 12 January. For all the fumblings around him, Bremner conducted affairs in midfield and jabbed away at a ponderous defence that was further ruffled by the good understanding Jordan and Jones had established.

Stronger sides would be less likely to succumb to a team that had not been at full strength since its opening salvo of seven successive victories. Draws at Everton (0-0) and at home to Chelsea (1-1) had to be ground out the hard way. On 6 February, Revie wrote to warn the nation that Leeds United could not always appear angelic. "We have been playing against teams with a grim determination to beat us. They fight and tackle harder against us than any other team."

When on 9 February, as Leeds left Old Trafford 2-0 victors over a Manchester United team propping up the first division, it was hard to see when, how or by whom the first defeat of Revie's team might be inflicted. They were now unbeaten in 29 league games, their lead over Liverpool was nine points. "It's all over bar the shouting," proclaimed the *News of the World*. It seemed as if the only danger to Leeds would come from believing such propaganda. Provided they remained vigilant and kept up good habits, there was nothing on the horizon to stop them but many a fine ship has been holed from below.

While Leeds had snuffed out the FA Cup challenge of Peterborough United, winning 4-1 at London Road with a first-half blitz of goals, their fifth-round opponents Bristol City were not to be disposed of so easily. Despite leading at Ashton Gate through a fierce, 25-yard shot by Bremner after 41 minutes, Leeds were harassed almost to breaking point by the energy and inventiveness of City's response. Only Harvey and the profligacy of Bristol's strikers saved the day and kept the score at 1-1. Perhaps Leeds thought Bristol had shot their bolt. Possibly they did not wish to be distracted by the FA Cup, for in the replay they were again outfought and out-thought and sunk deservedly, with 16 minutes left, by a single goal from Don Gillies.

For Leeds, only Hunter, Jones and Cooper – whose return, albeit fleeting, had delighted everyone – emerged with any credit.

After 19 minutes of their next league match at Stoke City, it looked as if all was well once more in Leeds United's world: smartly-taken goals by Clarke and Bremner had put them 2-0 up. Soon after, Leeds, already missing Jones, McQueen, Reaney and Gray, were to be robbed of Johnny Giles through a recurrence of the groin injury that had plagued him since the early season. Cooper, bravely though he tried, was no substitute and ill-equipped to deal with the counterthrust launched by Stoke midfielders Alan Hudson and John Mahoney, who could now scent a way back into the game. By half-time, Stoke had wiped out the deficit. Then, in the 67th minute, Leeds' unbeaten record of 29 league matches finally toppled as centre-half Denis Smith launched himself towards a corner kick and connected with a flying header that flew past Harvey and into the Leeds net. The match, already highly-charged, then became explosive as Leeds jettisoned their mild-mannered approach of autumn and responded with an alarming fury; the tackles reckless, the players as argumentative as ever they were in their wild past.

Revie's men found defeat hard to digest. They had also sustained a further casualty, David Harvey. Into the team for the next three matches came David Stewart, signed from Ayr United for £30,000 the previous October. Although the team had started to misfire badly, Stewart did not let them down: Leeds' deficiencies lay further upfield. Defeat at Stoke was followed by laborious 1-1 draws against Leicester and Newcastle, and a scratchy 1-0 home win over Manchester City that owed everything to an undeserved penalty, the fruit of Bremner's theatrical fall in the City area.

Liverpool meanwhile were stalking Revie's sickly team, the sound of their tread as heavy and portentous as was that of Arsenal in 1971. Leeds had averaged a point a game from their previous four outings; Liverpool had amassed seven. Suddenly their clash at Anfield on 16 March was invested with a new and awesome significance. A win for Leeds might yet keep them at bay. The prospect of defeat was too ghastly to contemplate but defeat there was. That it was a stirring game in the honourable tradition established by England's two finest teams was of little comfort to Revie's men. It was all the more painful because Leeds had fended off the Liverpool attack until seven minutes from time, Hunter once more shouldering a Herculean burden. As the Leeds defence lost a crucial battle for aerial supremacy, John Toshack headed down the ball for Steve Heighway to force the ball past David Harvey. Liverpool, with two games in hand, had now cut the lead of Revie's men to six points.

The team that had looked impregnable now seemed in a deep state of shock. Their preferred weapon in the home match against Burnley, who had long since faded from the championship race, was to hurl high balls then themselves towards goalkeeper Stevenson, who responded with a performance as brave as it was adroit. Between times, Leeds hesitated over shots, blundered in defence and Burnley scored four times. "Leeds were haunted by doubt, undermined by misunderstandings . . . their morale . . . even their reputation for manners on the verge of destruction," wrote Brian James in *The Sunday Times*.

Judged by the scoreline alone, Leeds' 3-1 defeat at West Ham suggested they might be heading for a complete breakdown. Once more, reporters had them on the psychiatrist's couch. "Leeds' emotions live close to the surface, their character constantly under stress from their own creativity, their persistent injury problems symptomatic not of damaged muscles but overstressed minds," wrote John Samuel in *The Guardian*. Again, they were violent and petulant in the last 20 minutes as the match ran away from them but they had shown a skill and coherence in the first half that recalled the mellow days of autumn, and taken the lead with a fine goal from Allan Clarke.

The arithmetic was more ominous than ever. For the first time all season, Leeds could now be overhauled by Liverpool who, if they won all their remaining games, could reach 66 points. The most Revie's men could hope for, with six games remaining, was 64. What had previously been almost unthinkable was now becoming the subject of morbid speculation.

Just as the vultures were gathering to feast on a spectacular collapse, Leeds dug deep into themselves. Their performance at home to Derby, too pitted with anxiety to be described as a backlash against their recent traumatic run, nevertheless indicated a retreat from panic and disorder. With Clarke suspended, Bremner, as so often, was the catalyst; his cunning lob instrumental in Leeds' first-half goal, scored by Lorimer, and clinching the match through his own athletic half-volley after 70 minutes. By then Derby, who had been stern, energetic opponents, were done for providing Leeds threw nothing away. They didn't.

The two points were like a raft to a drowning man. Two days later Liverpool, unbeaten in the league since Boxing Day, lost 1-0 to Sheffield United at Bramall Lane. A long-forgotten sense of optimism began to stir once more at Elland Road, though not sufficiently to replenish the confidence that had drained away. Leeds were a bag of nerves as they drew 0-0 at Coventry on 13 April, Easter Saturday, and no better in the goalless draw at Elland Road against Sheffield United two days later. Liverpool were unable to capitalise, dropping points in 1-1 draws at Manchester City and Ipswich.

Meanwhile, Revie was advocating three points for an away win. "The simple answer to defensive blockade," he said. It would also have been the answer to the pursuit of Liverpool; Leeds had won ten times on their travels, Liverpool only four. Here was a man without a sense of irony; some of Leeds United's finest hours had been built on defensive blockades.

There would be a dearth of pretty football over the last gruelling lap. It was to be a battle of mental strength with Leeds, haunted by so many failures at the last, having the greater struggle to come to terms with themselves. In his search for a combination that would fight to the last, Don Revie recalled Mick Jones, who had still not recovered fully from his knee injury when Leeds travelled to Bramall Lane the following night. They went in after a goalless first half, only to hear that Liverpool were 4-0 up against Manchester City at Anfield. Rather than go to pieces, Leeds marshalled themselves for a sustained assault on the suspect Sheffield defence. Peter Lorimer, so out of touch in recent weeks, forced a breakthrough on 58 minutes scoring from an acute drive after Jones' aerial presence caused disarray around the Sheffield goal. Once in front, Leeds stormed forward again. On 70 minutes, Mick Jones bore down on goal having taken on Lorimer's wily pass but was clattered to the ground in the penalty area by Micky Speight. Lorimer slammed home the spot-kick.

Suddenly, Leeds had a hand on the league title once more. Such was the unbounded joy of the travelling Leeds fans, one might have thought the championship already won. It was a sobering result for Liverpool for whom the run-in, so eagerly anticipated a month earlier, was now looking like hard labour. Leeds still had a battle with themselves to resolve but had surmounted a great psychological hurdle. It was a boost for when Ipswich Town came to do battle at Elland Road on 20 April.

There was to be none of the emollient assurance of the handsome victory at Portman Road in December. The stakes were too high; Ipswich too mobile and competitive to be anyone's stooges. They seemed instead to have come as tormenters. The effect of Leeds springing into an early two-goal lead thanks to a thunderous drive from Lorimer and an alert header from Bremner only provoked the visitors into unnervingly incisive football. Two-nil became 2-1 by half-time; 2-2 after 55 minutes. Elland Road fell morosely quiet. Another crisis threatened. Get up and at them . . . be quicker to the ball, came the frantic commands from the touchline. Leeds wound themselves up for another do or die assault. Twenty minutes remained when Allan Clarke bore down on the Ipswich goal. Did the ball hit his shoulder or his hand as he brought it under control? Ipswich manager Brian Robson claimed the latter but as Clarke smashed the ball into the net, the referee pointed to the centre circle. The ground was in tumult. As the last minutes ticked away there came a cacophonous noise from the masses populating the Gelderd End, then a chant of "Everton! Everton!" Rumours swept the terraces that Liverpool were losing at Goodison Park. If true, Leeds were about to win the championship. "It [the Leeds/Ipswich match] was not so much a game, more an emotional explosion," wrote Ken Jones in the *Sunday Mirror*. Rumour it was, though: Liverpool had held out

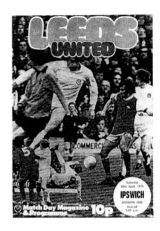

Rarely was a match approached with so much trepidation. Leeds' hopes of the 1973/74 League Championship hinged on this home match against Ipswich. Despite their faltering form, they won 3-2 on an afternoon of almost unbearable tension.

for a 0-0 draw but Leeds United's 3-2 win now meant that Liverpool, to overhaul them, had to win their remaining three matches even if Leeds lost their final game at Queen's Park Rangers.

Still the season had a final twist. Liverpool, unbeaten at home with 18 wins and just two draws, went out against Arsenal at Anfield four days later bristling with defiance. They besieged the Gunners' goal, creating chances galore, only to be vanquished by a solitary strike from Ray Kennedy on 55 minutes. Thanks to their old adversaries from north London, the travails of Don Revie and his men were over. At last the championship belonged to Leeds. That night, Revie had taken himself, his superstitions and some champagne to the home of a close friend. "Every time I do that, I get the right result and it has worked again," he declared.

The largest crowd in Loftus Road's history, 35,353, came out for the coronation. Leeds had been granted only 6,000 tickets: three times that number of their supporters seemed to find a way in, surging and swaying on the terraces like breaking waves, with gay abandon, living on their nerves no longer. In the end, Leeds had staggered to the league title but this game was a gentle reminder of what had brought them to it: brilliant long passes sprayed around by Bremner and Hunter, who had done so much to keep disintegration at bay in the traumatic finale; Giles busy and probing once more; then Clarke crowning the moment, finding space, taking Jordan's pass, and slotting home the ball with cool disdain to give his team a 1-0 win.

These were the good things that the country's finest football team was all about when free from the corrosive effects of self-doubt. For Jack Taylor, who had always maintained perfect control when refereeing some of their most important matches, Revie's team was uniquely gifted: "They were a beautifully balanced side. If they had played in another country and you put different coloured shirts on them and blacked their faces, I would still know it was Leeds."

POSTSCRIPT

There could be no more conclusive end to the Revie era. Finally, after his team's fabulous Indian Summer, he was lured away, unable to resist the job of England team manager. How triumphantly had Revie been justified in his belief that the weary troops who finished 1972/73 in such low spirits could renew themselves. Their performance in the first half of the championship campaign had been unsurpassable but it was unlikely they could do it again, for if Revie's hunger had been sated, by what means could he instill further ambition in players who had achieved so much?

Within a year of taking the England job, things started to go wrong for Revie. The sure touch he displayed within the intimacy of Elland Road deserted him in the colder, more formal England set-up. The England players were not his alone to mould, massage and drive almost to breaking point. He picked and dropped individuals quite arbitrarily, his judgement often swayed by a short-term burst of form. He lost the respect of others who sensed he was obsessional about money and too interested in pursuing commercial deals. With results and public opinion turning against him, Revie jumped ship in 1977. Convinced, probably correctly, that he was about to be sacked, he lined up a deal in the United Arab Emirates to run the national team.

The man who had been so gifted at public relations sullied his reputation permanently by selling his story to the *Daily Mail* before informing the Football Association. Various indignities were heaped over the once-proud Leeds manager's head. Allegations were published in the *Daily Mirror* claiming that Revie sought to bribe not only Bob Stokoe but, over the years, other players in an attempt to fix some of Leeds' most crucial games. Revie was then subjected to having his character assassinated in the High Court as the FA brought charges relating to breach of contract and deceitful conduct.

In the early 1980s, after returning from his relaxed and lucrative sojourn in Dubai, Revie had a role as paid consultant at Elland Road. He spent his later years in semi-retirement, playing golf and helping his son's sports promotions business before falling victim to motor neurone disease in 1986. He endured a traumatic final few years, becoming paralysed as his muscles wasted away, eventually dying on 26 May 1989. It was a tragic decline and fall.

Having ignored Revie's recommendations that Johnny Giles be appointed his successor, the Leeds board instead brought in Brian Clough. It was not so much a revolution, more 44 days of convulsions. From the day Clough told his new charges that they had won all their medals by cheating, he had a mutinous crew on his hands. With Bremner suspended following a fracas in the FA Charity Shield involving Kevin Keegan, Leeds made their worst start for years, winning only one and losing four of their first league matches. Clough departed rapidly. It had been an expensive and embarrassing six weeks.

Opposite. The Revie era is over and there is a turbulent figure at the head of the old guard: Brian Clough leads out his new charges for their Charity Shield match against Liverpool in August 1974.
Above. *It's the last straw for Billy Bremner – and Revie's old team, now managed by Jimmy Armfield – as Leeds are beaten by Bayern Munich in the 1975 European Cup Final.*
Below. *Jimmy Armfield*

Under new manager Jimmy Armfield, Leeds rediscovered some of their old momentum. Now, unquestionably a fading force, they still had the will and skill to reach the European Cup Final but the night of 28 May 1975 was another débâcle wherein the referee seemed less than even-handed and Leeds, who dominated almost throughout, lost to Bayern Munich with two late goals. There, in spirit, ended the Revie era. The fans' riotous behaviour in defeat was the harbinger of an ugly, new dark age.

Armfield presided over Leeds for almost four years, rebuilding with some skill. But the great old corps was irreplaceable and, although his teams were often attractive, the old passion and, of course, the results, were missing. The quality of Armfield's near misses never matched those of Revie's; nor were they interspersed with success.

That Leeds had become merely also-rans finally cost Armfield his job in July 1978. His successors, whether they stayed for a long time or short, sought in vain to recapture the glorious years. Jock Stein came and went in 44 days, lured away by the offer to manage the Scotland team. Jimmy Adamson came, prospered briefly, but made a clutch of misguided purchases and departed in September 1980 by popular demand. Allan Clarke, in his new guise as manager, talked a good job but, under his leadership, Leeds, now burdened with crippling debts as attendances plummeted, slid into the second division.

Above. Jock Stein
Below. Allan Clarke

The task of re-establishing Leeds in the top flight defeated his successors, Revie old boys Eddie Gray and Billy Bremner, though both, Bremner especially, came close. When Howard Wilkinson was appointed manager in October 1988, he was determined that the ghost of Revie be exorcised. Memorabilia of the Leeds godfather's era affixed to the foyer walls of Elland Road was banished. Prudently, but also with touches of inspiration, Wilkinson started to reconstruct the team. Eight years of exile from the first division ended on a hot afternoon in May 1990 when Leeds' 1-0 victory at Bournemouth gave them the second division championship.

Two years later, to the delight and astonishment of Leeds United aficianados, the first division championship was back at Elland Road. But not quite in the same old-fashioned way. It was less rancorous but there was less genius. It was won by fine, upstanding players but in the modern tradition and with freedom of contract. Most were imported, ready-made, and mature. They had not grown up together, many did not linger. Revie's players, on the other hand, seemed to march on in concert forever. Football had seen nothing like them beforehand. Nor will it again.

Above. Eddie Gray
Below. Jimmy Adamson

The Revie Era at a Glance

1960/61
14th in Division 2
FA Cup
Lost to Sheffield Wednesday in the 3rd round.
League Cup
Beat Blackpool and Chesterfield.
Lost to Southampton in the 4th round.

1961/62
19th in Division 2
FA Cup
Lost to Derby County.
League Cup
Beat Brentford and Huddersfield Town.
Lost to Rotherham United in the 4th-round replay.

1962/63
5th in Division 2
FA Cup
Beat Stoke City and Middlesbrough.
Lost to Nottingham Forest in the 5th round.
League Cup
Beat Crystal Palace.
Lost to Blackburn Rovers in the 3rd round.

1963/64
1st in Division 2
FA Cup
Beat Cardiff City.
Lost to Everton in the 4th-round replay.
League Cup
Beat Mansfield Town and Swansea Town.
Lost to Manchester City in the 4th round.

1964/65
2nd in Division 1
FA Cup
Beat Southport, Everton, Shrewsbury Town, Crystal Palace
and Manchester United.
Lost to Liverpool in the final.
League Cup
Beat Huddersfield Town.
Lost to Aston Villa in the 3rd round.

1965/66
2nd in Division 1
FA Cup
Beat Bury.
Lost to Chelsea in the 4th round.

Above. A sight to terrify any goalkeeper: an airborne Mick Jones moves in for the kill.
Opposite. A final triumph as an unforgettable era comes to an end. Don Revie had gone and the wilderness years were about to begin.

League Cup

Beat Hartlepool United.

Lost to West Bromwich Albion in the 3rd round.

Inter Cities Fairs Cup

Beat Torino, SC Leipzig, Valencia and Ujpest Dosza.

Lost to Real Zaragoza in the semi-final.

1966/67

4th in Division 1

FA Cup

Beat Crystal Palace, West Bromwich Albion, Sunderland
and Manchester City.

Lost to Chelsea in the semi-final.

League Cup

Beat Newcastle United and Preston North End.

Lost to West Ham United in the 4th round.

Inter Cities Fairs Cup

Beat DWS Amsterdam, Valencia, Bologna and Kilmarnock.

Lost to Dinamo Zagreb in the final.

1967/68

4th in Division 1

FA Cup

Beat Derby County, Nottingham Forest, Bristol City and
Sheffield United.

Lost to Everton in the semi-final.

League Cup Winners

Beat Luton Town, Bury, Sunderland, Stoke City, Derby
County and Arsenal in the final.

Inter Cities Fairs Cup Winners

Beat Spora Luxembourg, Partizan Belgrade, Hibernian,
Glasgow Rangers, Dundee and Ferencvaros in the final.

1968/69

1st in Division 1

FA Cup

Lost to Sheffield Wednesday in the 3rd round replay.

League Cup

Beat Charlton Athletic and Bristol City.

Lost to Crystal Palace in the 4th round.

Inter Cities Fairs Cup

Beat Standard Liège, Napoli, Hannover 96.

Lost to Ujpest Dosza in the 4th round.

1969/70

2nd in Division 1

FA Cup

Beat Swansea Town, Sutton United, Mansfield Town,
Swindon Town and Manchester United

Lost to Chelsea in the final replay

League Cup

Beat Fulham.

*Centre-half Roy Ellam was
bought from Huddersfield
Town but floundered in his
first season before returning
to his old club.*

Lost to Chelsea in the 3rd replay.
European Cup
Beat Lyn Oslo, Ferencvaros and Standard Liège.
Lost to Glasgow Celtic in the semi-final.

1970/71

2nd in Division 1
FA Cup
Beat Rotherham United and Swindon Town.
Lost to Colchester United in the 5th round.
League Cup
Lost to Sheffield United in the 2nd round.
Inter Cities Fairs Cup Winners
Beat Sarpsborg, Dynamo Dresden, Sparta Prague, Vitoria
Setubal, Liverpool and Juventus in the final.

1971/72

2nd in Division 1
FA Cup Winners
Beat Bristol Rovers, Liverpool, Cardiff City, Tottenham
Hotspur, Birmingham City and Arsenal in the final.
League Cup
Beat Derby County.
Lost to West Ham United in the 3rd-round replay.
UEFA Cup
Lost to Lierse SK in the 1st round.

1972/73

3rd in Division 1
FA Cup
Beat Norwich City, Plymouth Argyle, West Bromwich
Albion, Derby County and Wolverhampton Wanderers.
Lost to Sunderland in the final.
League Cup
Beat Burnley and Aston Villa.
Lost to Liverpool in the 4th round replay.
European Cup Winners Cup
Beat Ankaragucu, Carl Zeiss Jena, Rapid Bucharest,
Hajduk Split.
Lost to AC Milan in the final.

1973/74

1st in Division 1
FA Cup
Beat Wolverhampton Wanderers and Peterborough United.
Lost to Bristol City in the 5th-round replay.
League Cup
Lost to Ipswich Town in the 2nd round.
UEFA Cup
Beat Stromgodset Drammen, Hibernian.
Lost to Vitoria Setubal in the 3rd round.